Design Elements 5 by Ultimate Symbol

Published by Ultimate Symbol New York

Mies Hora

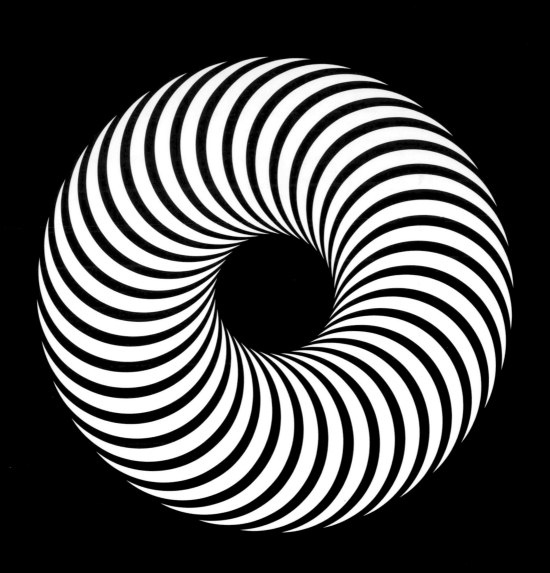

A fabulous and essential tool for any designer designing anything!
Paula Scher, Pentagram NY

Indispensable... wonderful!
Barbara Lee, Suka + Friends Design

Finest vector art library I've ever seen.
Terry Coleman, Visual Antics

This time-saver easily paid for itself after only a couple of uses.
Steff Geissbuhler, C+G Partners

Can't live without it... use it every week.
Kim Brill Graphic Design

Taxonomic, exhaustive quality to the organization and volume of images.
Glenn Fleishman, Adobe Magazine

Well executed and very convenient.
Dory Colbert Design

We use extensively.
Robert Buckingham, Department of Air Force

Worth every penny... used for countless logos.
Wes Wait Design

Wow!... the best resource I've ever seen on one disk.
Judith Thomas, Randolph-Macon Women's College

We love the quality.
Angela Nelson, Ernst & Young

Inspirational for both me and my students.
Lance Hidy, Professor of Design

Invaluable... the best ever... superb!
Timothy Holloway, Timage

Amazingly diverse array of scalable graphics... saves countless hours of time.
Betsy Binet, 2B Communications

Easy to use... I've used them 1,000 times.
Ellen Pettengell Design

Awesome!
Jennifer Zullo Design

Most useful collection I've ever bought.
Christian Boulad, Cejibe Communications

©2007 Ultimate Symbol
Library of Congress Control Number: 2007906127
ISBN: 978-0-9769513-1-5

First Edition paperback published in 1994
©1994 Ultimate Symbol

**Ultimate
Symbol**™

Published by
Ultimate Symbol
31 Wilderness Drive
Stony Point, New York 10980 USA
www.ultimatesymbol.com
800.611.4761 Sales & Upgrades
845.942.0004 Fax Orders
845.942.5342 Technical Support
845.942.0003 Business Office

Dedication This book is dedicated to Richard Hora, without whom this incredible journey would have never begun.

It is more than simply that he amassed the materials which were to serve as the foundation for *Design Elements*.

It was by witnessing my father at work in his design/painting studio, and eventually the privilege of working with him, that I learned something about the infinite exploration of seeing, meditation, taste, perseverance, and perhaps most importantly, discipline, in the act of creation. That I am the beneficiary of such gifts is why I am to him forever indebted.

Acknowledgements *Design Elements 5* was built upon the solid foundation of previous editions, the first of which was published in 1994. It is over a period of more than fourteen years that I have had the privilege to work with a remarkable group of visual professionals and individuals whose interest, skill, dedication, support, and sheer stamina enabled me to evolve this project into a 21st Century reference work. I am extremely grateful to everyone who has contributed to this formidable effort.

Mies Hora, *Concept, Design Director, Editor*
Richard Hora, *Project Consultant, Illustrator*
Frances Hora, *Project Assistant, Production Master*

Illustration / Design

Jen Alspach
Elizabeth Bakacs
Milan Bozic
Karl Llewellyn
Richard Manville
Craig Meachen
Chris O'Hara
Alan Weimer
Michael Wong
Joanna Zlowodzka

Special Thanks

Lou Dorfsman
David Freedman
Steff Geissbuhler
Jacqueline Hanley
Jill Joy
David C. Levy
Paula Scher

Design / Production

Roderick Cruz
David Caputo
Richard Day
Suzette DeNobriga-LeSage
Charlotte Felter
Alexandria Franco
Jane Jao
Paul Levy
Nicolle Marsilio
Kara Simeone
Alex Singleton
Paul Tu
Dorene Warner
Tai Lam Wong

Production Notes *Design Elements 5* and all of the images in it were designed and produced in Adobe Illustrator. This book is typeset in Univers. Printed and bound in China through Imago Sales USA

Cover and book design by Mies Hora

Table of Contents

Contents Continued 6

286 **Ordering & Upgrades
      How to Purchase
      Electronic Artwork for
      Images in this Book**
      All 5,025 images displayed
      in *Design Elements 5*
      are available as fully
      editable EPS vector image
      files for Mac or PC

Visual symbols are among the oldest permanent means of communication, dating back some 30,000 years to the caves of Lascaux and Altamira. Our ancestors included the shapes of arrows, hands, and geometric forms in their representations of bulls, horses and mammoths. Clearly those images fulfill some archetypal human need. Despite the distances we have traveled from those caves, we find that these same forms remain a compelling means for transmitting information. They are, today as then, an indispensable part of our visual language. In recent years, we have seen this tradition enriched by the signs of modern life – television screens, filmstrips, scientific nomenclature, etc.

The availability of a resource in which the very best of these images have been selected and exquisitely rendered for the purposes of reproduction is a great service to all of us, but it is most important to designers. The painstaking care with which Richard Hora and Mies Hora have undertaken this task is reflected in this collection, which represents an enormous research effort as well as the exercise of astute judgement, taste, and skill. Here is the highest level of visual quality and design utility. The thoughtfulness and comprehensive nature of their work makes this product invaluable for the concerned designer.

David C. Levy, Ph.D.
Former President, The Corcoran Gallery
Former Executive Dean, Parsons School of Design

A writer controls the content and elegance of his prose. Nevertheless, he is still at the mercy of his vocabulary. He can play with ideas, juggle ideas or parody ideas. He can sculpt paragraphs and say anything he feels like saying. But he can do none of this without words. They are his raw material, the source of his inspiration, the tools of his trade. A designer is not unlike a writer. His "words" are the graphic elements, symbols and signs which make up our common visual vocabulary. *Design Elements by Ultimate Symbol*, is an invaluable graphic reference work. It builds upon the sturdy foundation of the original four hard-cover books and

expands the designer's vocabulary to include an even more vast array of dingbats, designs, symbols, icons and calligraphic devices.

This extraordinary product provides the designer with a much-needed dictionary of images, a comprehensive resource for fine, reproduction quality ornaments and figures. Its immense practical value is matched only by its fine craftsmanship.

Lou Dorfsman
Former Vice President & Creative Director
Advertising & Design, CBS Inc.

Sometimes a designer starts with an idea and finds the visual form to express it. Other times the idea is triggered by visual input. The design process is a constant interplay between idea and form, form and idea. *Design Elements* provides a wealth of imagery with which to express ideas and is also a convenient visual resource from which ideas can grow. The carefully selected 'elements' in this compendium, including circles, suns, stars, arrows, and hearts, are truly 'elemental.' As we follow the author's thorough exploration of these forms from page to page, we are led naturally to an understanding of the forms themselves.

The quality, beauty, and utility of the selections in this rich compendium are only surpassed by the clarity of presentation and attention to detail. This incomparable reference provides a great foundation for graphic designers, and it is an indispensable addition to every design library.

David Freedman
Designer
formerly of Milton Glaser, Inc.

"What are you going to do with all of those files?", I asked, staring at a bank of black metal file cabinets. It was late 1979 and my father Richard, the consummate visual artist, was preparing to retire after a successful 40-year-long career in the graphic arts. Package design, calligraphy, industrial design, architectural and product design – he had done it all, and masterfully. Throughout the years he had meticulously filed his design work in those cabinets.

Innumerable variations of a particular design or theme were researched and developed for each project to satisfy both his clients and his own compulsive curiosity about visual forms and their relationships. The cumulative result was bewildering in volume and stunning in scope.

It would have been a shame not to make available such an exquisite and uniquely varied collection of visual ephemera, so I convinced him to publish it somehow and share the wealth.

Our goal was to edit and name the materials, carefully organize them into self-evident categories and, in effect, create a dictionary of visual forms. The task seemed daunting and it was. There were thousands of individual pieces of original artwork – stats, acetates, tracings, sketches, ink renderings, rapidograph noodlings, in addition to his extensive collection of old books, photographs, 19th-Century linecuts, engravings, German type specimens, and more. We decided to expand many categories with brand new material as well.

A comp was produced and a publisher was found. By 1981, Volumes 1 and 2, the first two of four hardcover volumes were published, entitled *Design Elements - A Visual Reference*. One decade and fifteen-thousand volume sales later, the digital world of CD-Rom's beckoned. What better way to reproduce and transmit our expanding visual reference than on a tiny, shiny disk?

Once again, father and son lay every last design element out on the floor, to reconfigure the collection for use on a computer, with all of the new capabilities that it affords. We re-edited the categories and added new ones to the collection in order to reflect yet another ten years of collection and creation, before painstakingly redrawing all of the elements in Adobe Illustrator.

I was looking for the ideal screen interface. One that would be intuitive and fun to use. Fortunately, Adobe Systems dropped in deux ex machina with their powerful Acrobat document software, which perfectly suited our product. At last, one can easily navigate the whole collection of thousands of images in minutes, locating any single category or specific symbol in seconds... now that's progress.

The visual arts and the design business truly have been changed forever by computers. In the process of design, a computer is only a tool, but it is a most efficient one. *Design Elements by Ultimate Symbol* is a testament to that fact. I hope that you use this labor of love well and in good taste. May it inform and inspire you, and save you precious time. For this designer, good design has always been good business. Even more importantly, good design is a source of great fun. Enjoy.

Mies Hora
President & Founder
Ultimate Symbol
1994

Mount Everest is climbed "because it is there".
The beauty of reaching the summit isn't only the epic physical reality that one can finally witness, but also the deep spiritual satisfaction acquired through the process of the climb. The lengthy, complex adventure of realizing this version of *Design Elements* feels like one more peak that has been reached on a continuing journey that reaches back more than twenty-eight years.

Designers have always been, by nature, inclined to create order wherever we find that it's in short supply. We also love to take a subject apart, preferably a new one, analyze and study it before the essential task of reassembly begins. This almost primal act of de-construction, organization, and clarification keeps our blood pulsing and our spirits fulfilled, our talents engaged and our minds challenged.

Design Elements 5 is the result of no less an obsessive process, a tantalizing journey into the limits of perse-verance, hope, and faith in the successful conclusion of a near "mission impossible". That is, to survey the ever expanding world of historical and modern visual ephemera in all of its shapes and forms: collect, create, assemble, archive, organize, render, catalog, and finally, present and publicize it.

When and how does one cease such an undertaking? The truth is that after many years of trying, one doesn't. The process of selecting and editing new material is infinite, so discipline was required to keep the project manageable. By the end, five new volumes and more than 2,000 new images were added to the previously published version. Every existing category was amended and extensive changes were made throughout to enhance the collection.

Every one of the 5,000 images in this collection originated in a drawing, a print, a sketch, as "scratch". Each was selected, edited, refined, scanned, then redrawn as a vector EPS. Great care was expended to choose which elements would be completely reconstructed as smooth

vectors, and which would remain in it's original rough-edged condition. The innate character of drawings, letterpress, metal or wood imprints of ink on paper is a large part of what makes some of this artwork so compelling, and retaining that quality is paramount. The playful freehand images in Volume 12 were particularly gratifying to create, if time-consuming to finalize. Capturing the spontaneity of brush strokes and ink splats is no simple matter.

Everything is individually printed, proofed, corrected, reprinted and approved before being layed out and catalogued with a number. All files are checked, have keywords associated with them, and are readied for digital reproduction and dissemination on CD and online.

This procedure required the tracking and handling, by a small army of individuals, of more than 30,000 items to finally bring the totality to a state of completion. All of this was, of course, quite formidable. But like many fellow and inveterate problem-solvers, I couldn't seem to help myself from jumping right into it all, again and again. Providing a uniquely rich, useful design resource for my peers, as well as for the general public, has been the greatest pleasure of all, another hard-won summit, the view from which it's a privilege to share.

Mies Hora
President & Founder
Ultimate Symbol
2007

About the Author Mies Hora founded the software content publishing firm Ultimate Symbol in 1992 and is responsible for directing the design, development, and marketing of the print and electronic versions of its growing library of titles. Mies coauthored a series of best-selling design reference books, *Design Elements 1, 2, 3,* and *4*, which were produced during 1980-85 in collaboration with his father, architect, designer and artist, Richard Hora. Ultimate Symbol digitized the book series and released *Design Elements by Ultimate Symbol* in 1994 as a catalog with CD in Mac/PC formats. Other titles currently include *Nature Icons, WebPage Graphics, Pictorial Symbols*, and the 2005 release of the landmark *Official Signs & Icons 2*. The internet has allowed Mies to reach a global design audience with his collections of visual material.

A graduate of Parsons School of Design, Mies has also been since 1979 the design director and principal of Hora Associates, where his experience includes positioning, corporate identity, advertising, product and interface design, web site design, publications and print media, packaging, photography, architectural signage, store display, and interior design. An Adjunct Professor at the State University of New York (SUNY) since 1996, he has received numerous awards for his work, and has been a longtime member of the American Institute of Graphic Arts, the Society for Environmental Graphic Design, and the International Interactive Communications Society.

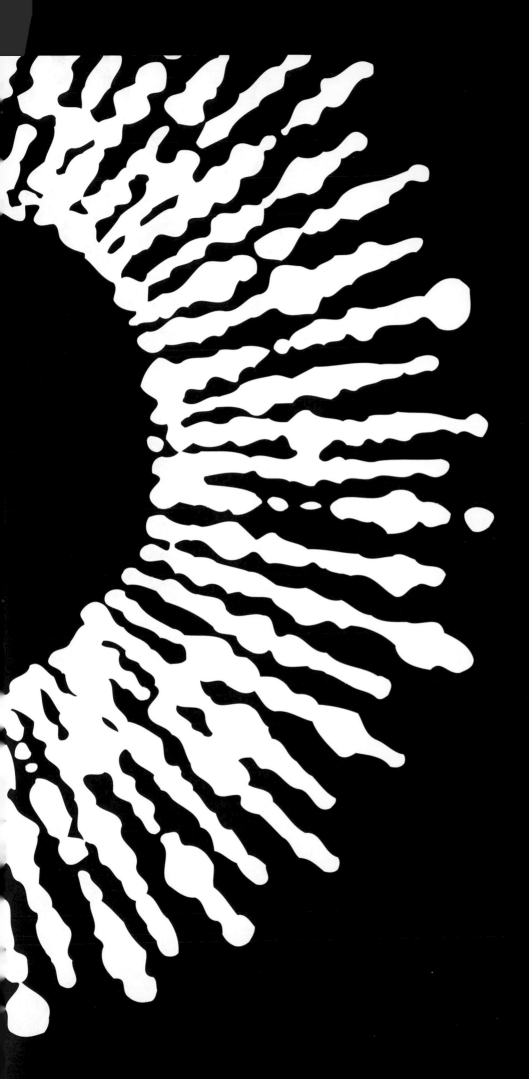

1

Suns
- Woodcut
- Drawn

D501**A**01

D501**A**02

D501**A**03

D501**A**04

D501**A**05

D501**A**08

D501**A**06

D501**A**07

D501**A**09

D501**A**10

D501**A**11

D501**A**12

D501**A**13

D501**A**14

D501**A**15

D501**A**16

D501**A**17

Suns
- Woodcut
- Drawn
  continued

D501**B**01

D501**B**02

D501**B**03

D501**B**04

D501**B**05

D501**B**06

D501**B**07

D501**B**08

D501**B**09

D501**B**10

D501**B**11

D501**B**12

D501**B**13

D501**B**14

D501**B**15

D501**B**16

D501**B**17

D501**B**18

D501**B**19

D501**B**20

Suns
- Drawn
  continued

D501**C**01   D501**C**02   D501**C**03   D501**C**04

D501**C**05   D501**C**06   D501**C**07   D501**C**08

D501**C**09   D501**C**10   D501**C**11   D501**C**12

D501**C**13   D501**C**14

Note: All images
are available as
fully editable vector
image files: see
page 286 or www.
ultimatesymbol.com

D501**C**15   D501**C**16   D501**C**17

Suns
- Drawn
  continued

D501**D**01

D501**D**02

D501**D**03

D501**D**04

D501**D**05

D501**D**06

D501**D**07

D501**D**08

D501**D**09

D501**D**10

D501**D**11

D501**D**12

D501**D**13

D501**D**14
Spanish Alchemy (Gold)

D501**D**15

D501**D**16
Spanish Cave

D501**D**17

Suns
- General

D501E01

D501E02

D501E03

D501E04

D501E05

D501E06

D501E07

D501E08

D501E09

D501E10

D501E11

D501E12

D501E13

D501E14

D501E15

D501E16

D501E17

Suns
- General
  continued

D501F01   D501F02   D501F03   D501F04

D501F05   D501F06   D501F07   D501F08

D501F09   D501F10   D501F11   D501F12

D501F13   D501F14   D501F15   D501F16

D501F17   D501F18   D501F19   D501F20
                      Ancient Sigil of the Sun

Suns
- General
  continued

D501**G**01

D501**G**02

D501**G**03

D501**G**04

D501**G**05

D501**G**06

D501**G**07

D501**G**08

D501**G**09

D501**G**10

D501**G**11

D501**G**12

D501**G**13

D501**G**14

D501**G**15

D501**G**16

D501**G**17

Suns
- General
continued

D501H01

D501H02

D501H03

D501H04

D501H05

D501H06

D501H07

D501H08

D501H09

D501H10

D501H11

D501H12

D501H13

D501H14

D501H15

D501H16
Pre-Columbian Ecuador

D501H17

Suns
- General
  continued

D501**J**01

D501**J**02

D501**J**03

D501**J**04

D501**J**05

D501**J**06

D501**J**07

D501**J**08

D501**J**09

D501**J**10

D501**J**11

D501**J**12

D501**J**13

D501**J**14

D501**J**15

D501**J**16

D501**J**17

D501**J**18

D501**J**19

D501**J**20

Suns
- General
continued

D501**K**01

D501**K**02

D501**K**03

D501**K**04

D501**K**05

D501**K**06

D501**K**07

D501**K**08

D501**K**09

D501**K**10

D501**K**11

D501**K**12

D501**K**13

D501**K**14

D501**K**15

D501**K**16

D501**K**17

Suns
- General
continued

D501L01

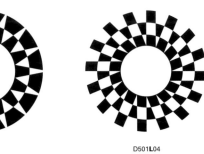

D501L02

D501L05

D501L03

D501L04

D501L06

D501L07

D501L08

D501L09

D501L10

D501L11

D501L12

D501L13
Rising Sun
National Symbol of Japan

D501L14

D501L15

D501L16

D501L17

Suns
- General
  continued

D501M01

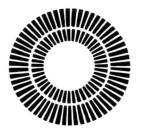

D501M02

D501M03

D501M04

D501M05

D501M06

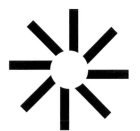

D501M07

D501M08

D501M09

D501M10

D501M11

D501M12

- Rise

D501M13

D501M14

D501M15

D501M16

D501M17

D501M18

D501M19

D501M20

Suns
- Faces

D501N01

D501N02

D501N03
Venetian

D501N04
German

D501N05

D501N06

D501N07

D501N08

D501N09
German

D501N10

D501N11

D501N12
German

D501N13

Moons
- Faces

D501N14

D501N15

D501N16

D501N17

Moons
- Faces
  continued

D501**P**01

D501**P**02

D501**P**03

D501**P**04

D501**P**05

D501**P**06

D501**P**07

D501**P**08

D501**P**09

D501**P**10

D501**P**11

D501**P**12

D501**P**13

D501**P**14

D501**P**15

D501**P**16

D501**P**17

D501**P**18

D501**P**19

D501**P**20

Moons
- Phases

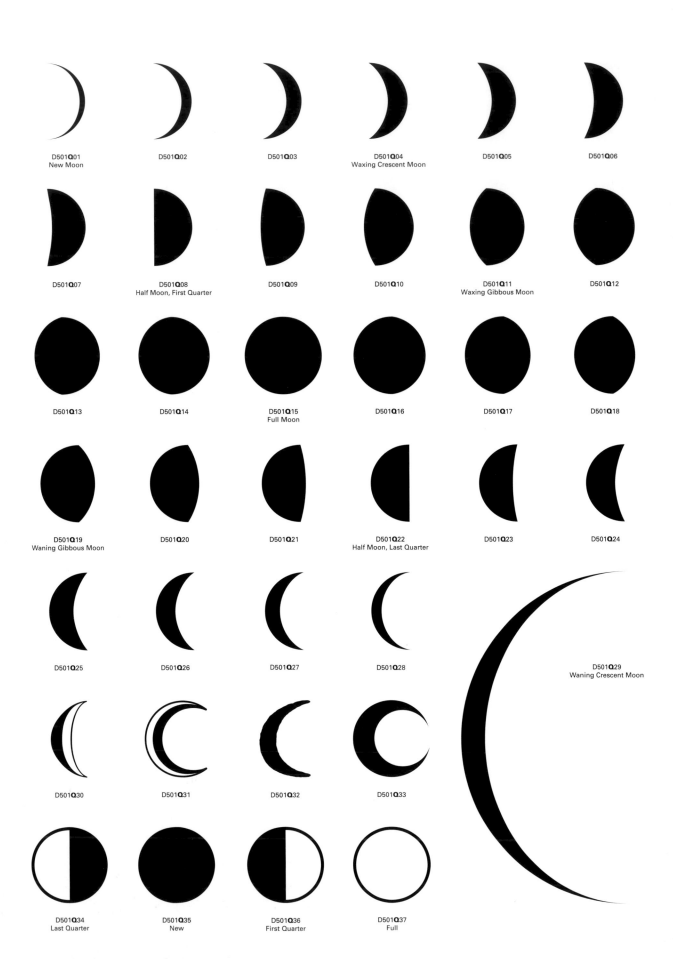

D501Q01
New Moon

D501Q02

D501Q03

D501Q04
Waxing Crescent Moon

D501Q05

D501Q06

D501Q07

D501Q08
Half Moon, First Quarter

D501Q09

D501Q10

D501Q11
Waxing Gibbous Moon

D501Q12

D501Q13

D501Q14

D501Q15
Full Moon

D501Q16

D501Q17

D501Q18

D501Q19
Waning Gibbous Moon

D501Q20

D501Q21

D501Q22
Half Moon, Last Quarter

D501Q23

D501Q24

D501Q25

D501Q26

D501Q27

D501Q28

D501Q29
Waning Crescent Moon

D501Q30

D501Q31

D501Q32

D501Q33

- Phase
 Symbols

D501Q34
Last Quarter

D501Q35
New

D501Q36
First Quarter

D501Q37
Full

Planetary

Astronomy
- Symbols

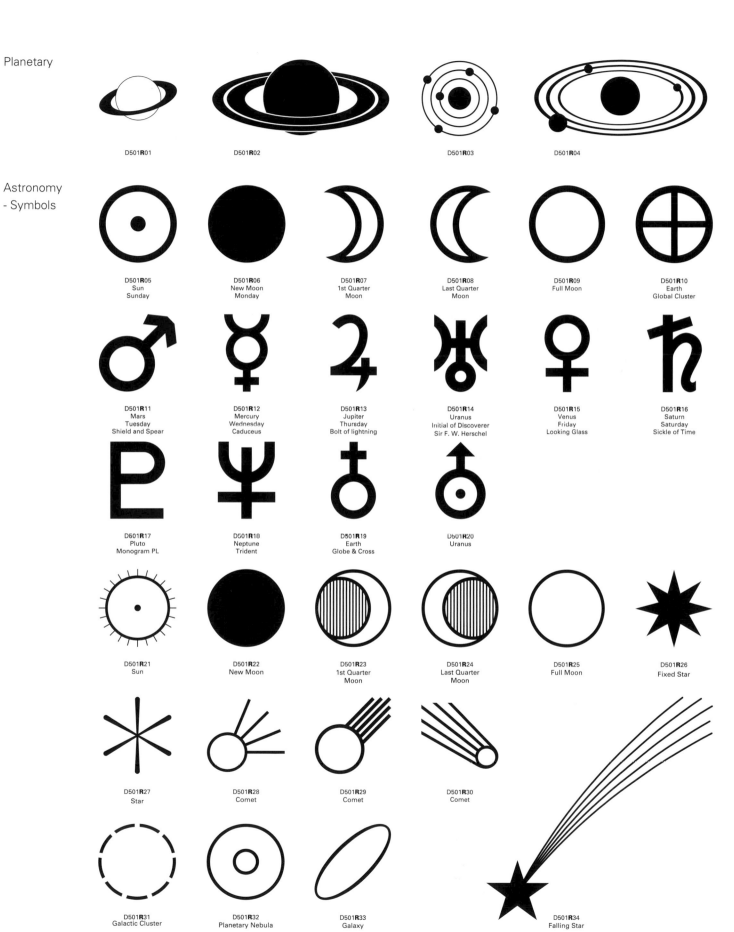

D501R01

D501R02

D501R03

D501R04

D501R05
Sun
Sunday

D501R06
New Moon
Monday

D501R07
1st Quarter
Moon

D501R08
Last Quarter
Moon

D501R09
Full Moon

D501R10
Earth
Global Cluster

D501R11
Mars
Tuesday
Shield and Spear

D501R12
Mercury
Wednesday
Caduceus

D501R13
Jupiter
Thursday
Bolt of lightning

D501R14
Uranus
Initial of Discoverer
Sir F. W. Herschel

D501R15
Venus
Friday
Looking Glass

D501R16
Saturn
Saturday
Sickle of Time

D501R17
Pluto
Monogram PL

D501R18
Neptune
Trident

D501R19
Earth
Globe & Cross

D501R20
Uranus

D501R21
Sun

D501R22
New Moon

D501R23
1st Quarter
Moon

D501R24
Last Quarter
Moon

D501R25
Full Moon

D501R26
Fixed Star

D501R27
Star

D501R28
Comet

D501R29
Comet

D501R30
Comet

D501R31
Galactic Cluster

D501R32
Planetary Nebula

D501R33
Galaxy

D501R34
Falling Star

Astronomy
- Aspects & Nodes

D501**S**01
Conjunction

D501**S**02
Ascending Node
The Dragon's Head

D501**S**03
Descending node
The Dragon's Tail

D501**S**04
Opposition

D501**S**05
Quadrature-Half

D501**S**06
Quadrature

- Positions

D501**S**07
Quadrante-
One and a Half

D501**S**08
Quintile

D501**S**09
Quincunx

D501**S**10
Sextile

D501**S**11
Sextile-Half

D501**S**12
Trine

D501**S**13
Sun's
Center

D501**S**14
Sun's
Upper Limb

D501**S**15
Sun's
Lower Limb

D501**S**16
Moon's
Upper Limb

D501**S**17
Moon's
Lower Limb

D501**S**18
Station Mark

- Time

D501**S**19
Hour

D501**S**20
Day

D501**S**21
Week

D501**S**22
Month

D501**S**23
Year

D501**S**24
Day & Night

Astrology

501**S**25
Horoscope

Astrology
Zodiac Symbols

D501**T**01
Aries
March 21
Vernal Equinox

D501**T**02
Taurus
April 20

D501**T**03
Gemini
May 21

D501**T**04
Cancer
June 21
Summer Solstice

D501**T**05
Leo
July 23

D501**T**06
Virgo
August 23

D501**T**07
Libra
September 23
Autumnal Equinox

D501**T**08
Scorpio
October 23

D501**T**09
Sagittarius
November 20

D501**T**10
Capricorn
December 21

D501**T**11
Aquarius
January 20

D501**T**12
Pisces
February 18

D501**T**13
Ram

D501**T**14
Bull

D501**T**15
Twins

D501**T**16
Lobster

D501**T**17
Lion

D501**T**18
Virgin

D501**T**19
Balance

D501**T**20
Scorpian

Astrology
Zodiac Symbols
continued

D501**U**01
Archer

D501**U**02
Goat

D501**U**03
Water Bearer

D501**U**04
Fishes

D501**U**05
Ram

D501**U**06
Bull

D501**U**07
Twins

D501**U**08
Crab

D501**U**09
Lion

D501**U**10
Virgin

D501**U**11
Balance

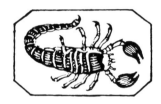

D501**U**12
Scorpion

D501**U**13
Archer

D501**U**14
Goat

D501**U**15
Water Bearer

D501**U**16
Fishes

D501**U**17
Ram

D501**U**18
Bull

D501**U**19
Twins

D501**U**20
Lobster

Astrology
Zodiac Symbols
continued

D501**V**01
Lion

D501**V**02
Virgin

D501**V**03
Balance

D501**V**04
Scorpion

D501**V**05
Archer

D501**V**06
Goat

D501**V**07
Water Bearer

D501**V**08
Fishes

D501**V**09
Ram

D501**V**10
Bull

D501**V**11
Twins

D501**V**12
Crab

D501**V**13
Lion

D501**V**14
Virgin

D501**V**15
Balance

D501**V**16
Scorpian

D501**V**17
Archer

D501**V**18
Goat

D501**V**19
Water Bearer

D501**V**20
Fishes

Astrology
Zodiac Symbols
continued

D501**W**01
Ram

D501**W**02
Bull

D501**W**03
Twins

D501**W**04
Crab

D501**W**05
Lion

D501**W**06
Virgin

D501**W**07
Balance

D501**W**08
Scorpion

D501**W**09
Archer

D501**W**10
Goat

D501**W**11
Water Bearer

D501**W**12
Fishes

D501**W**13
Aries

D501**W**14
Taurus

D501**W**15
Gemini

D501**W**16
Cancer

D501**W**17
Leo

D501**W**18
Virgo

D501**W**19
Libra

D501**W**20
Scorpio

Astrology
Zodiac Symbols
continued

D501**X**01
Sagittarius

D501**X**02
Capricorn

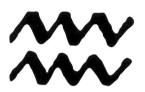

D501**X**03
Aquarius

D501**X**04
Pisces

D501**X**05
Aries

D501**X**06
Taurus

D501**X**07
Gemini

D501**X**08
Cancer

D501**X**09
Leo

D501**X**10
Virgo

D501**X**11
Libra

D501**X**12
Scorpio

D501**X**15
Sagittarius

D501**X**13
Capricorn

D501**X**14
Aquarius

D501**X**16
Pisces

Stars
- 5 Point
  continued

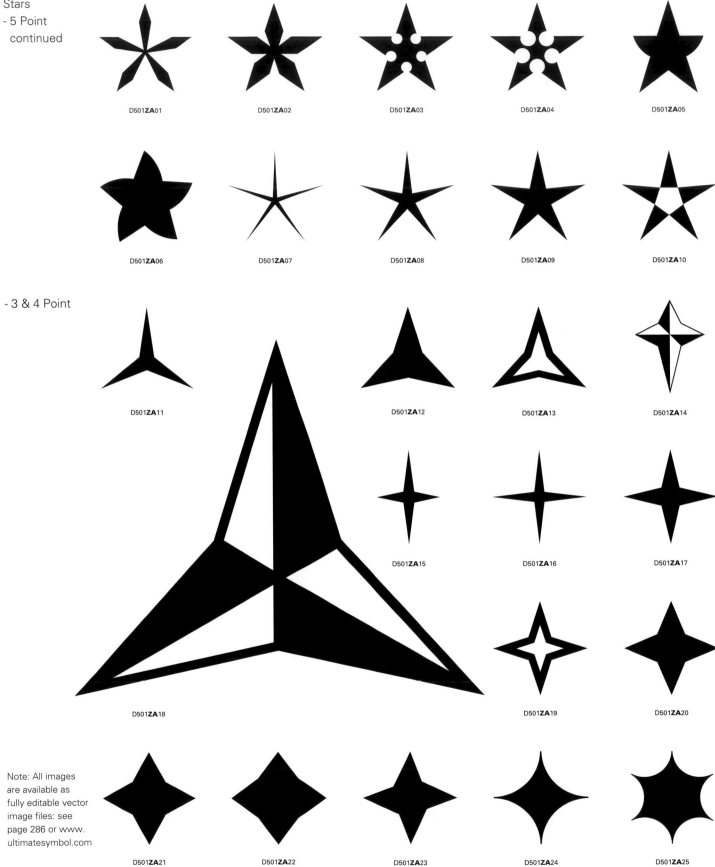

D501**ZA**01   D501**ZA**02   D501**ZA**03   D501**ZA**04   D501**ZA**05

D501**ZA**06   D501**ZA**07   D501**ZA**08   D501**ZA**09   D501**ZA**10

- 3 & 4 Point

D501**ZA**11   D501**ZA**12   D501**ZA**13   D501**ZA**14

D501**ZA**15   D501**ZA**16   D501**ZA**17

D501**ZA**18   D501**ZA**19   D501**ZA**20

Note: All images
are available as
fully editable vector
image files: see
page 286 or www.
ultimatesymbol.com

D501**ZA**21   D501**ZA**22   D501**ZA**23   D501**ZA**24   D501**ZA**25

Stars
- 6 & 7 Point

D501**ZB**01

D501**ZB**02

D501**ZB**03
Star of David

D501**ZB**04
Star of David
Mogen David

D501**ZB**05
Star of David

D501**ZB**06

D501**ZB**07

D501**ZB**08

D501**ZB**09

D501**ZB**10

D501**ZB**11

D501**ZB**12

D501**ZB**13

D501**ZB**14

D501**ZB**15

D501**ZB**16
Heptagram
Mystic Star

D501**ZB**17

- 8 Point

D501**ZB**18

D501**ZB**19

D501**ZB**20

D501**ZB**21

D501**ZB**22

Stars
- 8 Point
  continued

D501**ZC**01

D501**ZC**02

D501**ZC**03

D501**ZC**04
Star of Regeneration

D501**ZC**05

D501**ZC**06

D501**ZC**07

D501**ZC**08

D501**ZC**09

D501**ZC**10
Octagram of Creation

D501**ZC**11

D501**ZC**12

D501**ZC**13

D501**ZC**14

D501**ZC**15

- Multi-point

D501**ZC**16

D501**ZC**17

D501**ZC**18

D501**ZC**19

Stars
- Multi-point
continued

D501**ZD**01
10 Point
Ten Disciples of Jesus

D501**ZD**02

D501**ZD**03

D501**ZD**04

D501**ZD**05

D501**ZD**06

D501**ZD**07

D501**ZD**08

D501**ZD**09

D501**ZD**10
12 Point

D501**ZD**11
12 Point

D501**ZD**12
12 Point

D501**ZD**13
12 Point
The Twelve Tribes of Israel

D501**ZD**14
12 Point

D501**ZD**15
14 Point

D501**ZD**16

D501**ZD**17

D501**ZD**18

D501**ZD**19

D501**ZD**20

D501**ZD**21

D501**ZD**22

2

Spencerian
Initial Caps

D502**A**01
A

D502**A**02
A alternate

D502**A**03
B

D502**A**04
C

D502**A**05
D

D502**A**06
E

D502**A**07
F

D502**A**08
G

D502**A**09
H

D502**A**10
I

D502**A**11
J

D502**A**12
K

D502**A**13
K alternate

D502**A**14
L

D502**A**15
M

D502**A**16
N

D502**A**17
N alternate

Spencerian
Initial Caps
continued

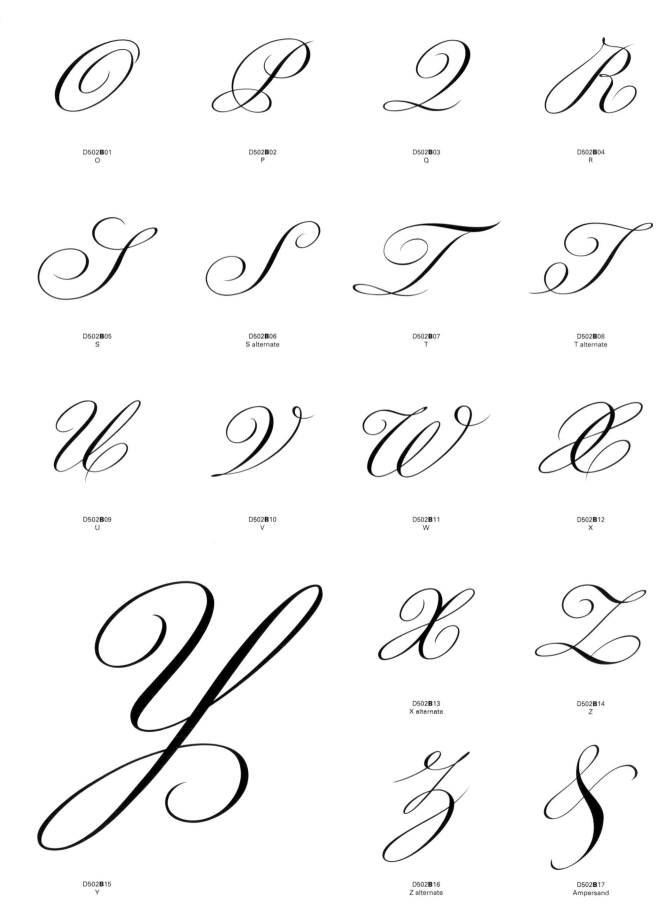

D502**B**01
O

D502**B**02
P

D502**B**03
Q

D502**B**04
R

D502**B**05
S

D502**B**06
S alternate

D502**B**07
T

D502**B**08
T alternate

D502**B**09
U

D502**B**10
V

D502**B**11
W

D502**B**12
X

D502**B**13
X alternate

D502**B**14
Z

D502**B**15
Y

D502**B**16
Z alternate

D502**B**17
Ampersand

Spencerian
Flourishes
Accents

D502**C**01   D502**C**02

D502**C**03   D502**C**04   D502**C**05   D502**C**06

D502**C**07   D502**C**08   D502**C**09   D502**C**10

D502**C**11   D502**C**12   D502**C**13   D502**C**14

D502**C**15   D502**C**16   D502**C**17   D502**C**18

Note: All images
are available as
fully editable vector
image files: see
page 286 or www.
ultimatesymbol.com

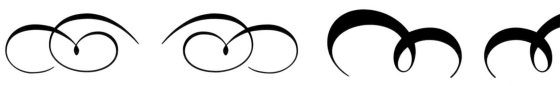

D502**C**19   D502**C**20   D502**C**21   D502**C**22

Spencerian
Flourishes
Accents
continued

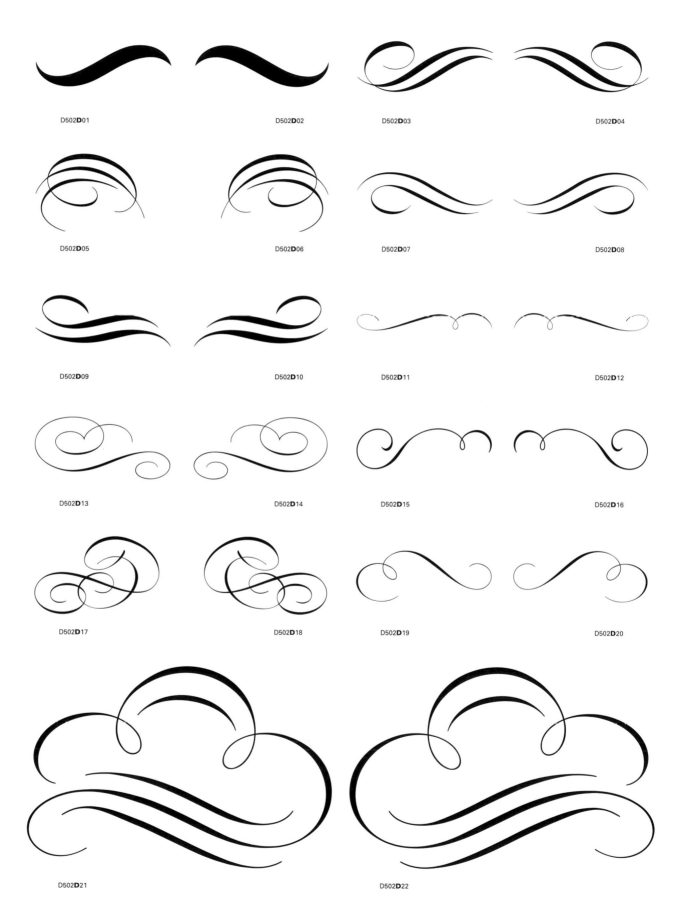

D502**D**01

D502**D**02

D502**D**03

D502**D**04

D502**D**05

D502**D**06

D502**D**07

D502**D**08

D502**D**09

D502**D**10

D502**D**11

D502**D**12

D502**D**13

D502**D**14

D502**D**15

D502**D**16

D502**D**17

D502**D**18

D502**D**19

D502**D**20

D502**D**21

D502**D**22

Spencerian
Flourishes
Accents
continued

D502E01

D502E02

D502E03

D502E04

D502E05

D502E06

D502E07

D502E08

D502E09

D502E10

D502E11

D502E12

D502E13

D502E14

D502E15

D502E16

D502E17

D502E18

D502E19

D502E20

D502E21

D502E22

Spencerian
Flourishes
Accents
continued

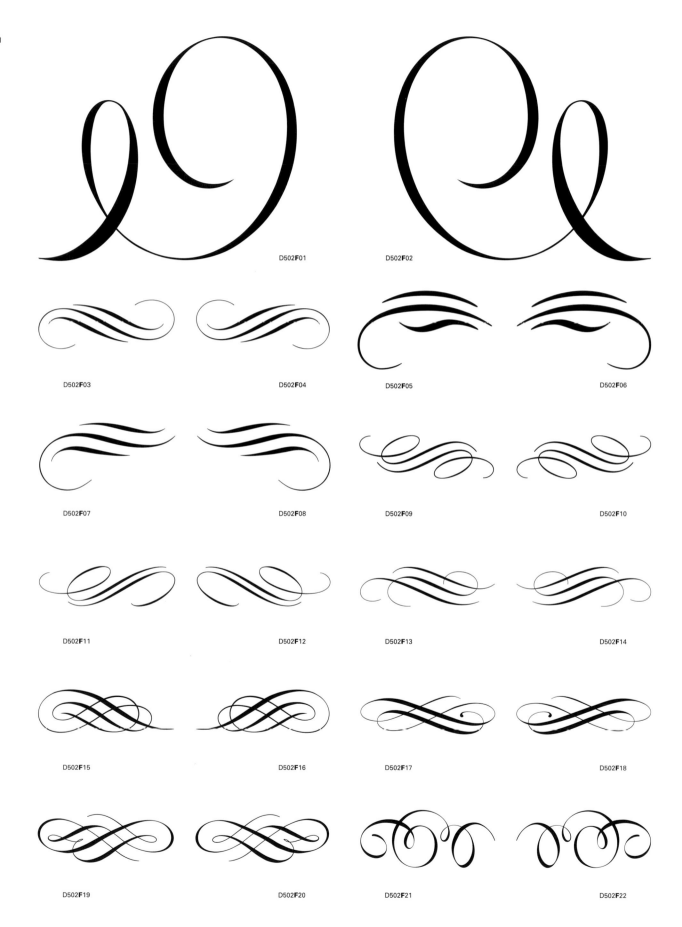

D502F01

D502F02

D502F03

D502F04

D502F05

D502F06

D502F07

D502F08

D502F09

D502F10

D502F11

D502F12

D502F13

D502F14

D502F15

D502F16

D502F17

D502F18

D502F19

D502F20

D502F21

D502F22

Spencerian
Flourishes
Accents
continued

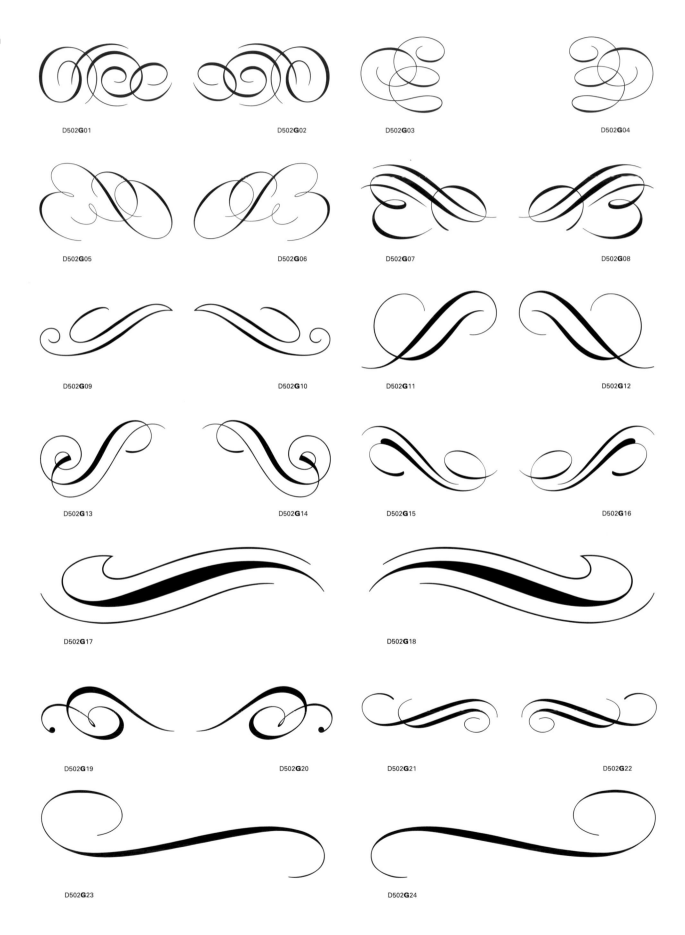

D502**G**01

D502**G**02

D502**G**03

D502**G**04

D502**G**05

D502**G**06

D502**G**07

D502**G**08

D502**G**09

D502**G**10

D502**G**11

D502**G**12

D502**G**13

D502**G**14

D502**G**15

D502**G**16

D502**G**17

D502**G**18

D502**G**19

D502**G**20

D502**G**21

D502**G**22

D502**G**23

D502**G**24

Spencerian
Flourishes
Accents
continued

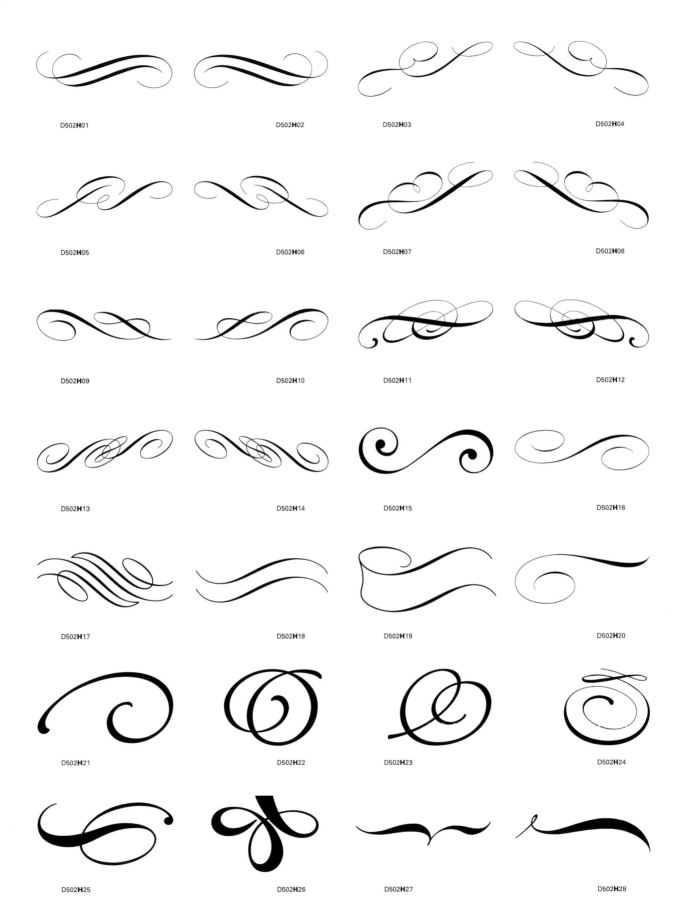

D502H01 D502H02 D502H03 D502H04

D502H05 D502H06 D502H07 D502H08

D502H09 D502H10 D502H11 D502H12

D502H13 D502H14 D502H15 D502H16

D502H17 D502H18 D502H19 D502H20

D502H21 D502H22 D502H23 D502H24

D502H25 D502H26 D502H27 D502H28

Spencerian
Flourishes
Accents
continued

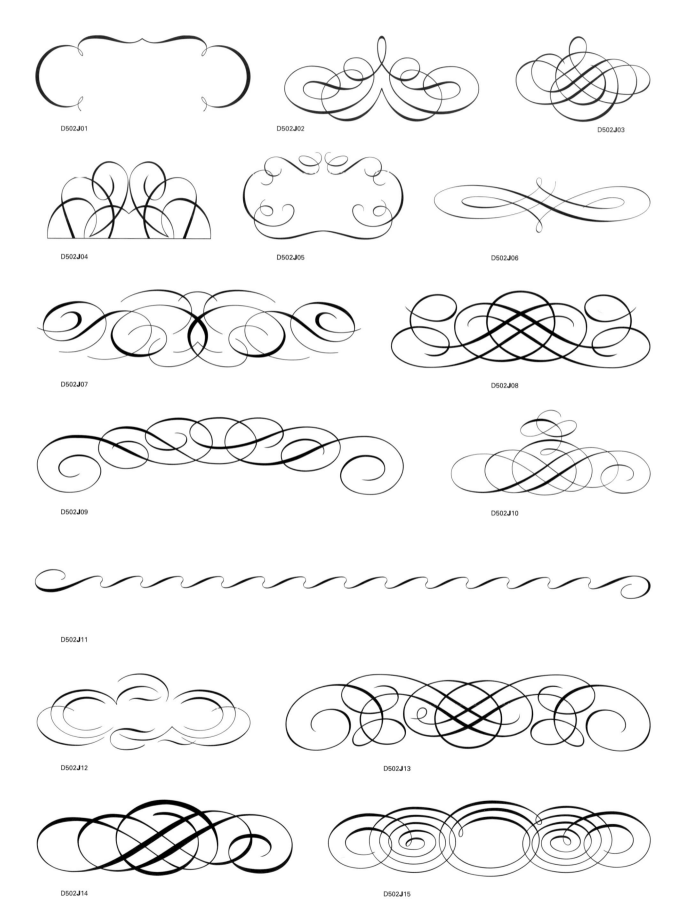

D502J01

D502J02

D502J03

D502J04

D502J05

D502J06

D502J07

D502J08

D502J09

D502J10

D502J11

D502J12

D502J13

D502J14

D502J15

Spencerian
Flourishes
Accents
continued

D502**K**01

D502**K**02

D502**K**03

D502**K**04

D502**K**05

D502**K**06

D502**K**07

D502**K**08

D502**K**09

D502**K**10

D502**K**11

D502**K**12

D502**K**13

D502**K**14

D502**K**15

D502**K**16

D502**K**17

D502**K**18

D502**K**19

D502**K**20

D502**K**21

Spencerian
Flourishes
Accents
continued

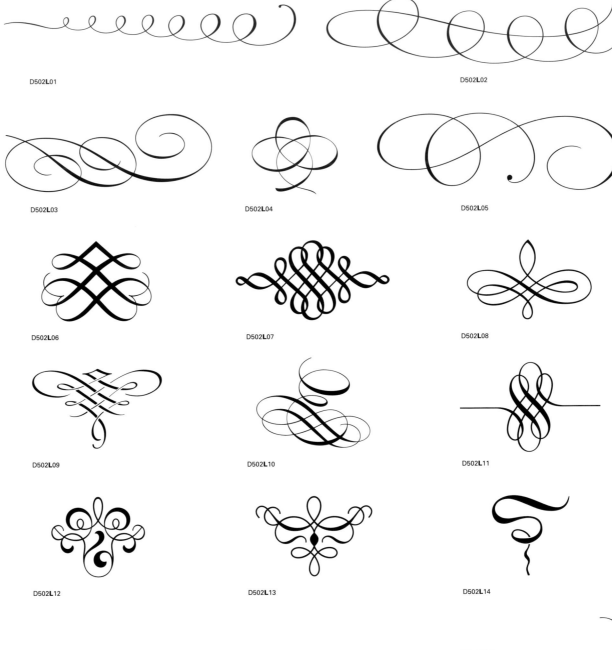

D502L01

D502L02

D502L03

D502L04

D502L05

D502L06

D502L07

D502L08

D502L09

D502L10

D502L11

D502L12

D502L13

D502L14

D502L15

D502L16

Spencerian
Flourishes
Accents
continued

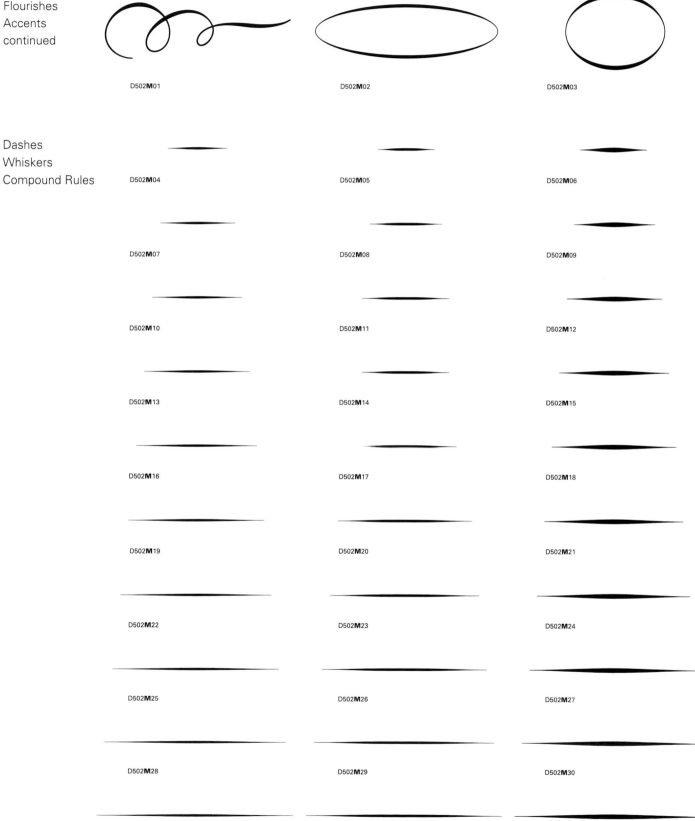

D502**M**01

D502**M**02

D502**M**03

Dashes
Whiskers
Compound Rules

D502**M**04

D502**M**05

D502**M**06

D502**M**07

D502**M**08

D502**M**09

D502**M**10

D502**M**11

D502**M**12

D502**M**13

D502**M**14

D502**M**15

D502**M**16

D502**M**17

D502**M**18

D502**M**19

D502**M**20

D502**M**21

D502**M**22

D502**M**23

D502**M**24

D502**M**25

D502**M**26

D502**M**27

D502**M**28

D502**M**29

D502**M**30

D502**M**31

D502**M**32

D502**M**33

Dashes
Whiskers
Compound Rules
continued

D502**N**01

D502**N**02

D502**N**03

D502**N**04

D502**N**05

D502**N**06

D502**N**07

D502**N**08

D502**N**09

D502**N**10

D502**N**11

D502**N**12

D502**N**13

D502**N**14

D502**N**15

D502**N**16

D502**N**17

D502**N**18

D502**N**19

D502**N**20

D502**N**21

D502**N**22

D502**N**23

D502**N**24

Dashes
Whiskers
Compound Rules
continued

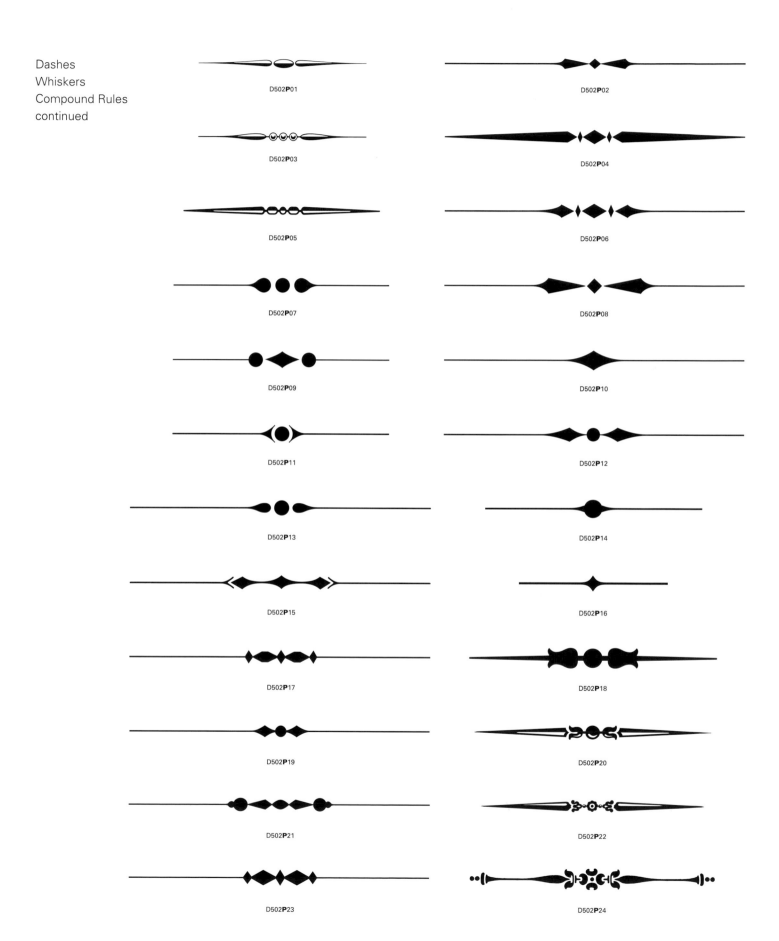

D502**P**01

D502**P**02

D502**P**03

D502**P**04

D502**P**05

D502**P**06

D502**P**07

D502**P**08

D502**P**09

D502**P**10

D502**P**11

D502**P**12

D502**P**13

D502**P**14

D502**P**15

D502**P**16

D502**P**17

D502**P**18

D502**P**19

D502**P**20

D502**P**21

D502**P**22

D502**P**23

D502**P**24

Dashes
Whiskers
Compound Rules
continued

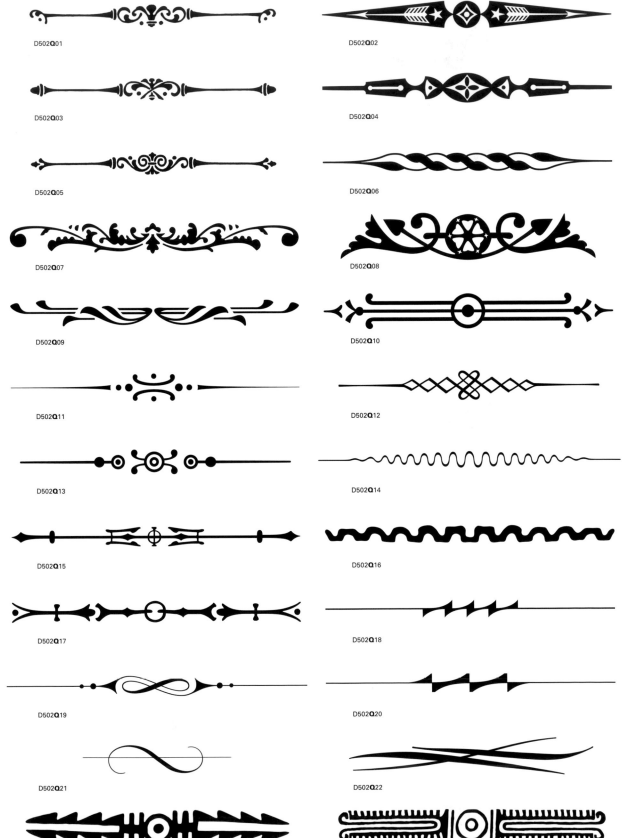

D502Q01

D502Q02

D502Q03

D502Q04

D502Q05

D502Q06

D502Q07

D502Q08

D502Q09

D502Q10

D502Q11

D502Q12

D502Q13

D502Q14

D502Q15

D502Q16

D502Q17

D502Q18

D502Q19

D502Q20

D502Q21

D502Q22

D502Q23

D502Q24

Dashes
Whiskers
Compound
Rules
continued

D502**R**01

D502**R**02

D502**R**03

D502**R**04

D502**R**05

D502**R**06

D502**R**07

D502**R**08

D502**R**09

D502**R**10

D502**R**11

D502**R**12

D502**R**13

D502**R**14

D502**R**15

D502**R**16

D502**R**17

D502**R**18

D502**R**19

D502**R**20

Dashes
Whiskers
Compound
Rules
continued

D502**S**01   D502**S**02   D502**S**03

D502**S**04   D502**S**05   D502**S**06

D502**S**07   D502**S**08   D502**S**09   D502**S**10

D502**S**11   D502**S**12   D502**S**13

D502**S**14   D502**S**15   D502**S**16   D502**S**17

D502**S**18   D502**S**19

D502**S**20   D502**S**21   D502**S**22   D502**S**23   D502**S**24   D502**S**25

Dashes
Whiskers
Compound
Rules
continued

D502T01   D502T02   D502T03

D502T04   D502T05   D502T06

D502T07   D502T08   D502T09

D502T10   D502T11   D502T12

D502T13   D502T14   D502T15

D502T16   D502T17   D502T18

D502T19   D502T20   D502T21

Typographic
Accents
Paragraph
Breaks

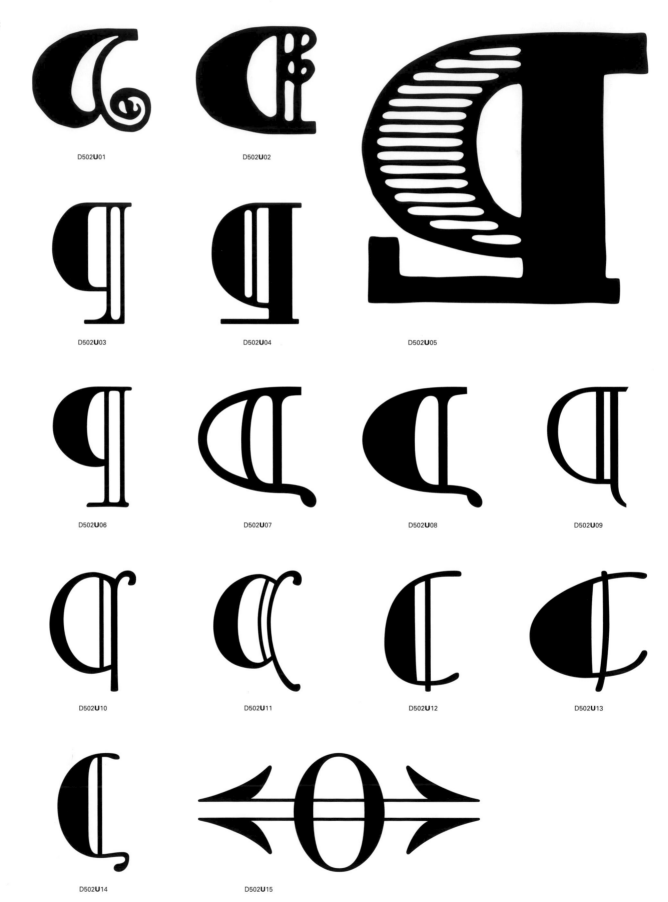

D502**U**01   D502**U**02

D502**U**03   D502**U**04   D502**U**05

D502**U**06   D502**U**07   D502**U**08   D502**U**09

D502**U**10   D502**U**11   D502**U**12   D502**U**13

D502**U**14   D502**U**15

Brackets
Braces
Parentheses

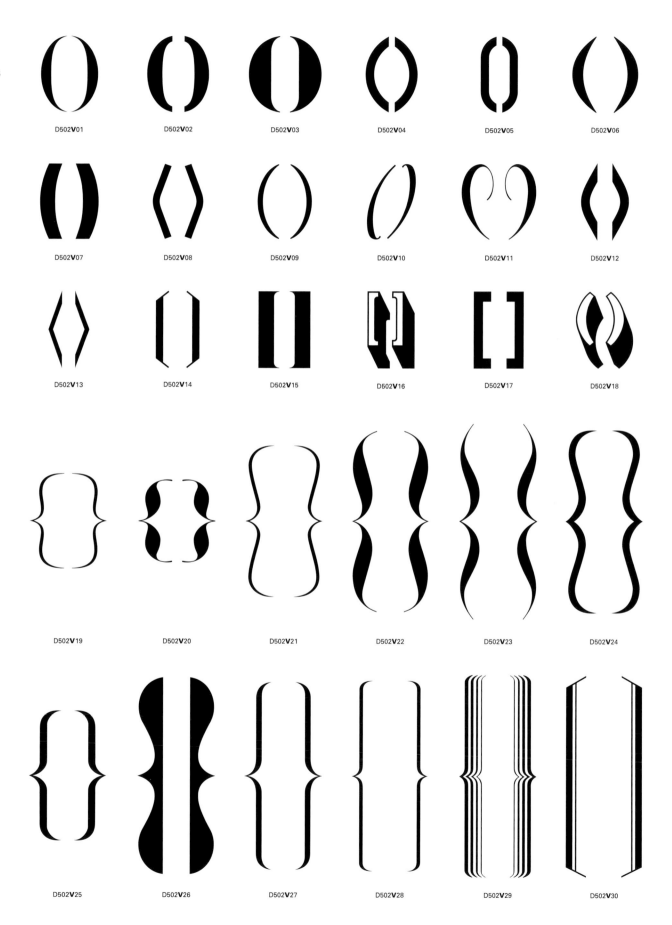

D502**V**01   D502**V**02   D502**V**03   D502**V**04   D502**V**05   D502**V**06

D502**V**07   D502**V**08   D502**V**09   D502**V**10   D502**V**11   D502**V**12

D502**V**13   D502**V**14   D502**V**15   D502**V**16   D502**V**17   D502**V**18

D502**V**19   D502**V**20   D502**V**21   D502**V**22   D502**V**23   D502**V**24

D502**V**25   D502**V**26   D502**V**27   D502**V**28   D502**V**29   D502**V**30

Brackets
Braces
Parentheses
continued

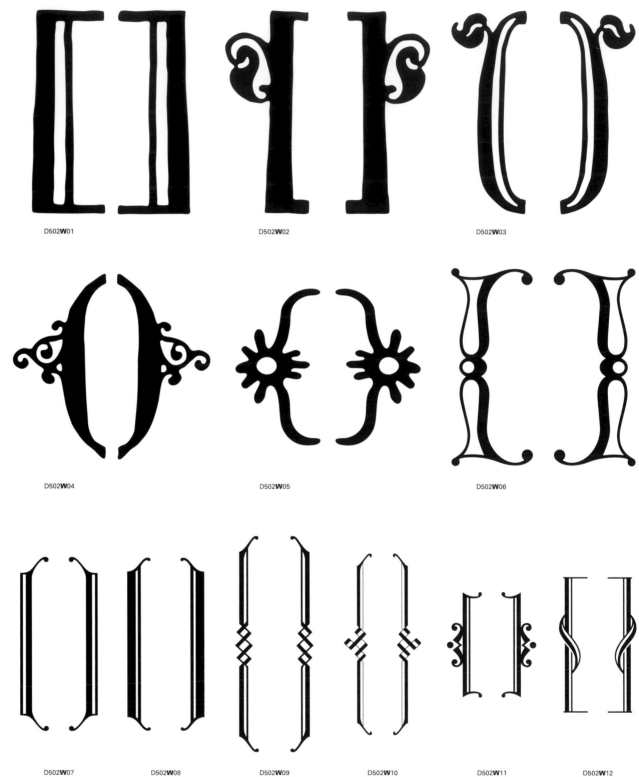

D502**W**01   D502**W**02   D502**W**03

D502**W**04   D502**W**05   D502**W**06

D502**W**07   D502**W**08   D502**W**09   D502**W**10   D502**W**11   D502**W**12

Note: All images
are available as
fully editable vector
image files: see
page 286 or www.
ultimatesymbol.com

Brackets
Braces
Parentheses
continued

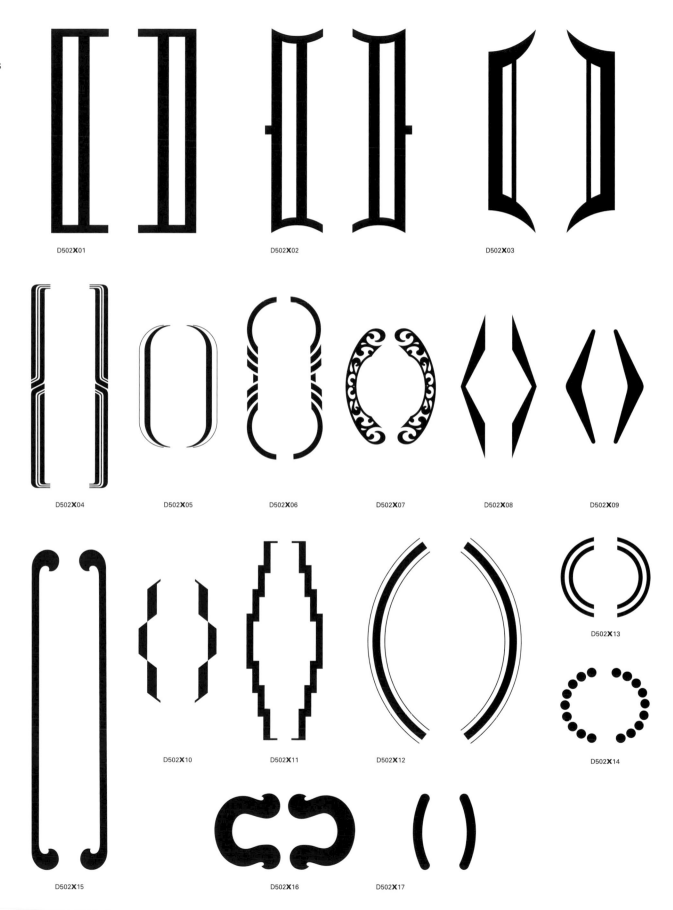

D502**X**01

D502**X**02

D502**X**03

D502**X**04

D502**X**05

D502**X**06

D502**X**07

D502**X**08

D502**X**09

D502**X**13

D502**X**10

D502**X**11

D502**X**12

D502**X**14

D502**X**15

D502**X**16

D502**X**17

3

Varied Weight

- Scotch

D503**A**01

D503**A**02

D503**A**03

D503**A**04

D503**A**05

D503**A**06

D503**A**07

D503**A**08

D503**A**09

D503**A**10

D503**A**11

D503**A**12

D503**A**13

D503**A**14

D503**A**15

D503**A**16

D503**A**17

D503**A**18

D503**A**19

D503**A**20

D503**A**21

D503**A**22

D503**A**23

Geometric
- Rectangles

D503**B**01

D503**B**02

D503**B**03

D503**B**04

D503**B**05

D503**B**06

D503**B**07

D503**B**08

D503**B**09

D503**B**10

D503**B**11

D503**B**12

D503**B**13

D503**B**14

D503**B**15

D503**B**16

D503**B**17

D503**B**18

D503**B**19

D503**B**20

D503**B**21

D503**B**22

D503**B**23

Geometric
- Rectangles
continued

D503**C**01

D503**C**02

D503**C**03

D503**C**04

D503**C**05

D503**C**06

- Circles

D503**C**07

D503**C**08

D503**C**09

D503**C**10

D503**C**11

D503**C**12

D503**C**13

D503**C**14

D503**C**15

D503**C**16

D503**C**17

D503**C**18

D503**C**19

D503**C**20

D503**C**21

Note: All images
are available as
fully editable vector
image files: see
page 286 or www.
ultimatesymbol.com

D503**C**22

D503**C**23

Geometric
continued
- Triangles

D503**D**01

D503**D**02

D503**D**03

D503**D**04

D503**D**05

D503**D**06

D503**D**07

D503**D**08

- Diamonds

D503**D**09

D503**D**10

D503**D**11

D503**D**12

D503**D**13

D503**D**14

D503**D**15

D503**D**16

D503**D**17

D503**D**18

D503**D**19

D503**D**20

D503**D**21

D503**D**22

D503**D**23

Ornate

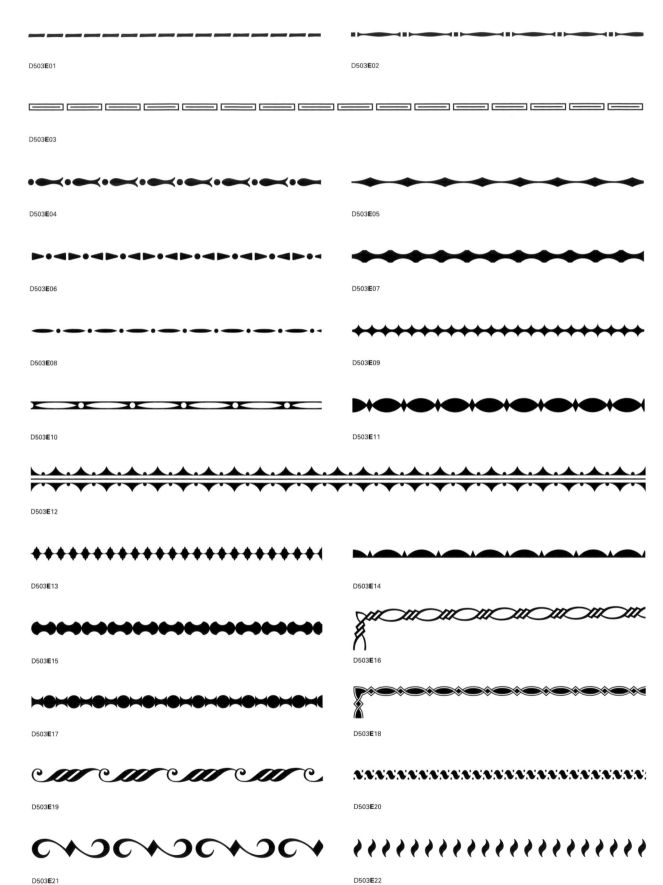

D503E01

D503E02

D503E03

D503E04

D503E05

D503E06

D503E07

D503E08

D503E09

D503E10

D503E11

D503E12

D503E13

D503E14

D503E15

D503E16

D503E17

D503E18

D503E19

D503E20

D503E21

D503E22

Ornate
continued

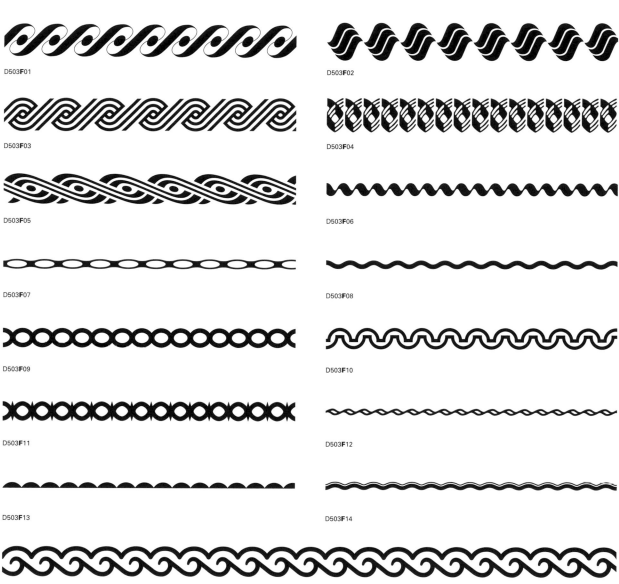

D503F01

D503F02

D503F03

D503F04

D503F05

D503F06

D503F07

D503F08

D503F09

D503F10

D503F11

D503F12

D503F13

D503F14

D503F15

D503F16

D503F17

D503F18

D503F19

D503F20

D503F21

D503F22

Ornate
continued

D503**G**01

D503**G**02

D503**G**03

D503**G**04

D503**G**05

D503**G**06

D503**G**07

D503**G**08

D503**G**09

D503**G**10

D503**G**11

D503**G**12

D503**G**13

D503**G**14

D503**G**15

D503**G**16

- Art Nouveau

D503**G**17

D503**G**18

D503**G**19

D503**G**20

D503**G**21

D503**G**22

Ornate
- Art Nouveau
continued

D503H01

D503H02

D503H03

D503H04

D503H05

D503H06

D503H07

D503H08

D503H09

D503H10

D503H11

D503H12

D503H13

D503H14

D503H15

D503H16

D503H17

D503H18

D503H19

D503H20

Ornate
continued
- Classical

D503J01

D503J02

D503J03

D503J04

D503J05

D503J06

D503J07

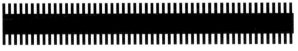

D503J08

D503J09

- Pre-Columbian

D503J10

D503J11

D503J12

D503J13

D503J14

D503J15

D503J16

D503J17

D503J18

D503J19

D503J20

D503J21

D503J22

D503J23

Ornate
continued
- Pre-Columbian
- Early Mexican

D503**K**01

D503**K**02

D503**K**03

D503**K**04

D503**K**05

D503**K**06

D503**K**07

D503**K**08

D503**K**09

D503**K**10

D503**K**11

D503**K**12

D503**K**13

D503**K**14

D503**K**15

D503**K**16

D503**K**17

D503**K**18

D503**K**19

D503**K**20

Ornate
continued
- Geometric

D503L01

D503L02

D503L03

D503L04

D503L05

D503L06

D503L07

D503L08

D503L09

D503L10

D503L11

D503L12

D503L13

D503L14

D503L15

D503L16

D503L17

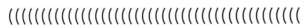

D503L18

D503L19

D503L20

D503L21

D503L22

Ornate
continued

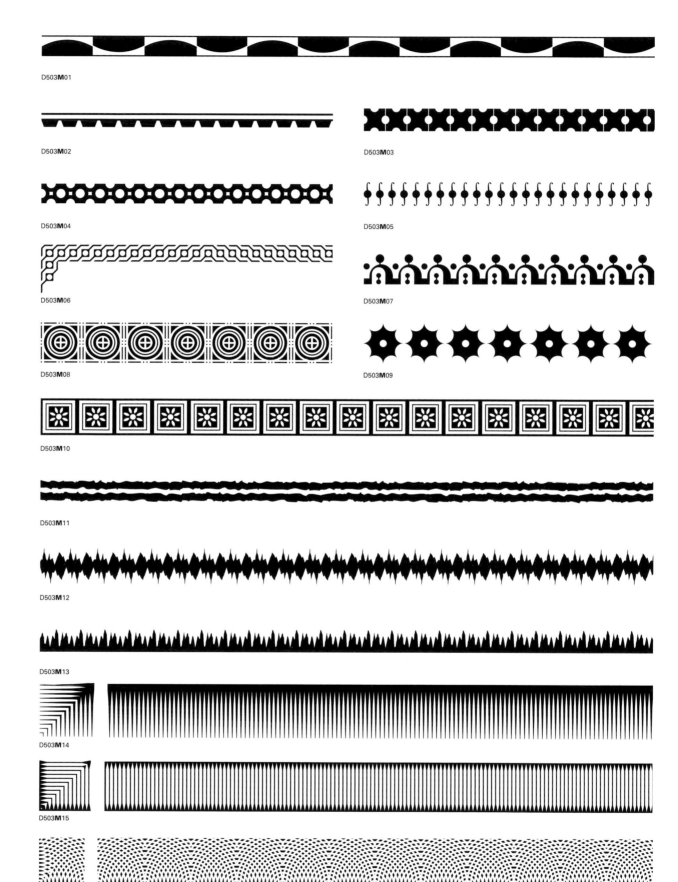

D503**M**01

D503**M**02

D503**M**03

D503**M**04

D503**M**05

D503**M**06

D503**M**07

D503**M**08

D503**M**09

D503**M**10

D503**M**11

D503**M**12

D503**M**13

D503**M**14

D503**M**15

D503**M**16

Ornate
continued
- Floral

D503N01

D503N02

D503P03

D503N04

D503N05

D503N06

D503N07

D503N08

D503N09

D503N10

D503N11

D503N12

D503N13

D503N14

D503N15

D503N16

D503N17

D503N18

D503N19

D503N20

D503N21

D503N22

D503N23

Ornate
continued
- Floral

D503**P**01   Oak and Acorn

D503**P**02

D503**P**03

D503**P**04

D503**P**05

D503**P**06

D503**P**07

D503**P**08

D503**P**09

D503**P**10

D503**P**11

D503**P**12

D503**P**13

D503**P**14

D503**P**15

D503**P**16

D503**P**17

D503**P**18

D503**P**19

Ornate
continued
- Floral

D503Q01

D503Q02

D503Q03

D503Q04

D503Q05

D503Q06

D503Q07

D503Q08

D503Q09   Holly

D503Q10   Holly

D503Q11   Holly

D503Q12   Holly

Pictorial

D503Q13   Barbed Wire

D503Q14   Rope

D503Q15   Rope

D503Q16   Rope

D503Q17   Braid

D503Q18   Rope

Note: All images
are available as
fully editable vector
image files: see
page 286 or www.
ultimatesymbol.com

D503Q19   Braid

D503Q20   Braid

Ornate
continued
- Pictorial

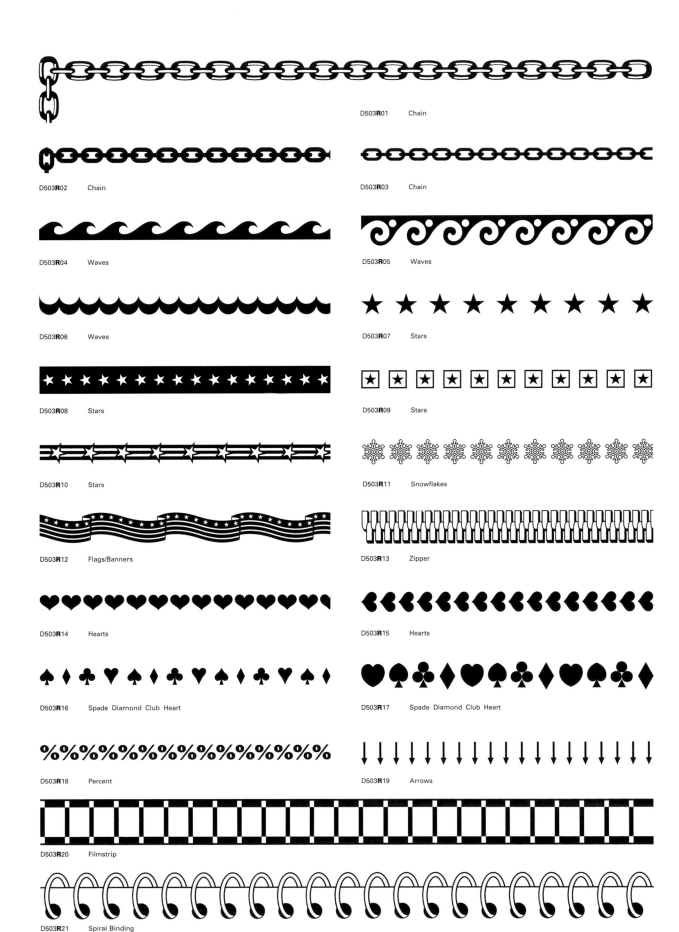

D503**R**01   Chain

D503**R**02   Chain

D503**R**03   Chain

D503**R**04   Waves

D503**R**05   Waves

D503**R**06   Waves

D503**R**07   Stars

D503**R**08   Stars

D503**R**09   Stars

D503**R**10   Stars

D503**R**11   Snowflakes

D503**R**12   Flags/Banners

D503**R**13   Zipper

D503**R**14   Hearts

D503**R**15   Hearts

D503**R**16   Spade Diamond Club Heart

D503**R**17   Spade Diamond Club Heart

D503**R**18   Percent

D503**R**19   Arrows

D503**R**20   Filmstrip

D503**R**21   Spiral Binding

4

Ribbons
Bows
Bowties

D504**A**01

D504**A**02

D504**A**03

D504**A**06

D504**A**04

D504**A**05

D504**A**07

D504**A**08

D504**A**09

D504**A**10

D504**A**11

D504**A**12

D504**A**13

D504**A**15

D504**A**16

D504**A**14

D504**A**17

D504**A**18

D504**A**19

D504**A**20

D504**A**21

D504**A**22

D504**A**23

Ribbons
Bows
Bowties
continued

Gifts

D504B01

D504B02

D504B03

D504B04

D504B05

D504B06

D504B07

D504B08

D504B09

D504B10

D504B11

D504B12

D504B14

D504B13

D504B15

D504B16

D504B17

D504B18
Support Ribbon
Charity

Filmstrips

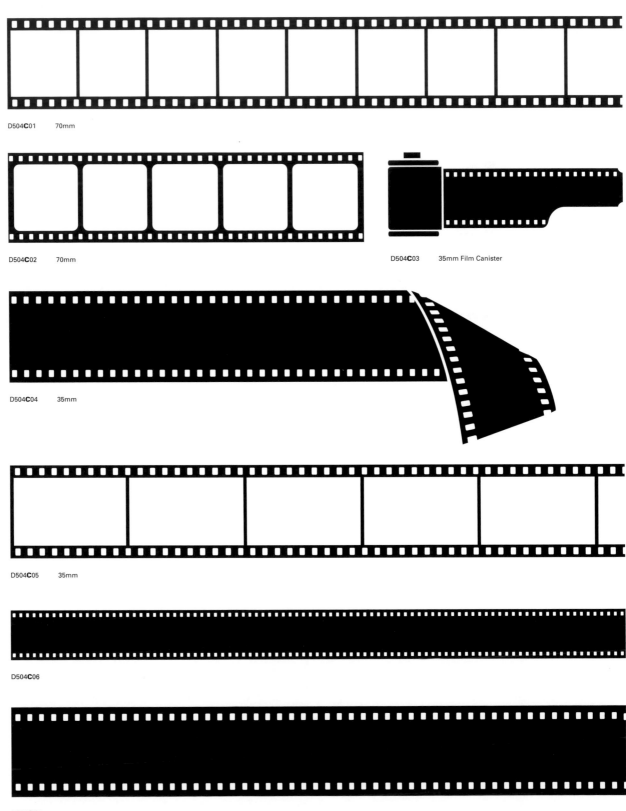

D504**C**01   70mm

D504**C**02   70mm

D504**C**03   35mm Film Canister

D504**C**04   35mm

D504**C**05   35mm

D504**C**06

D504**C**07

D504**C**08

Note: All images
are available as
fully editable vector
image files: see
page 286 or www.
ultimatesymbol.com

Tags
Hang Tags
Labels

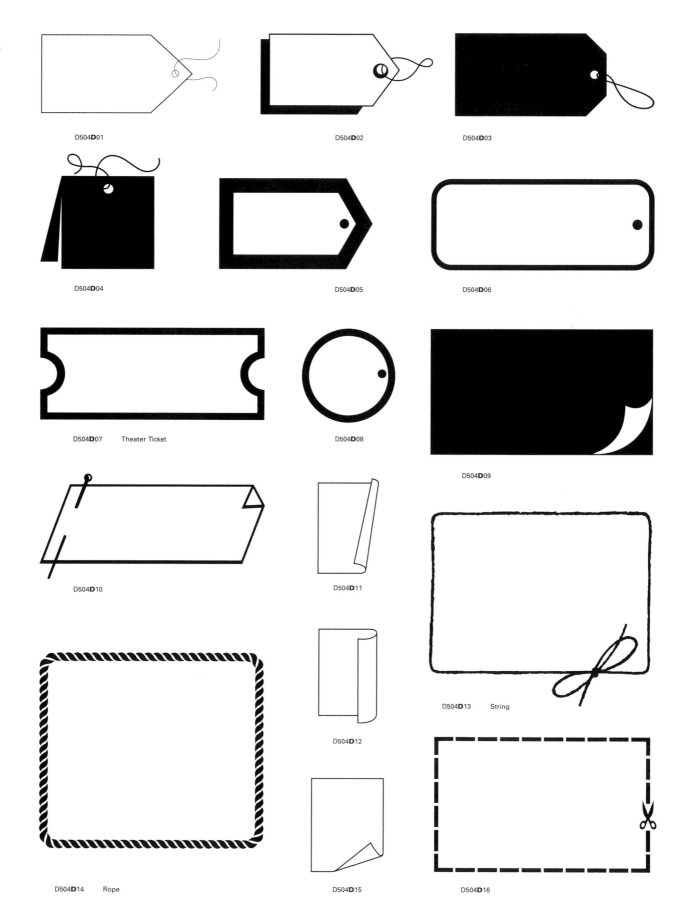

D504**D**01

D504**D**02

D504**D**03

D504**D**04

D504**D**05

D504**D**06

D504**D**07   Theater Ticket

D504**D**08

D504**D**09

D504**D**10

D504**D**11

D504**D**12

D504**D**13   String

D504**D**14   Rope

D504**D**15

D504**D**16

Seals

D504E01

D504E02

D504E03

D504E04

D504E05

D504E06

D504E07

D504E08

D504E09

D504E10

D504E11

D504E12

D504E13

D504E14

D504E15

D504E16

D504E17

Seals
continued

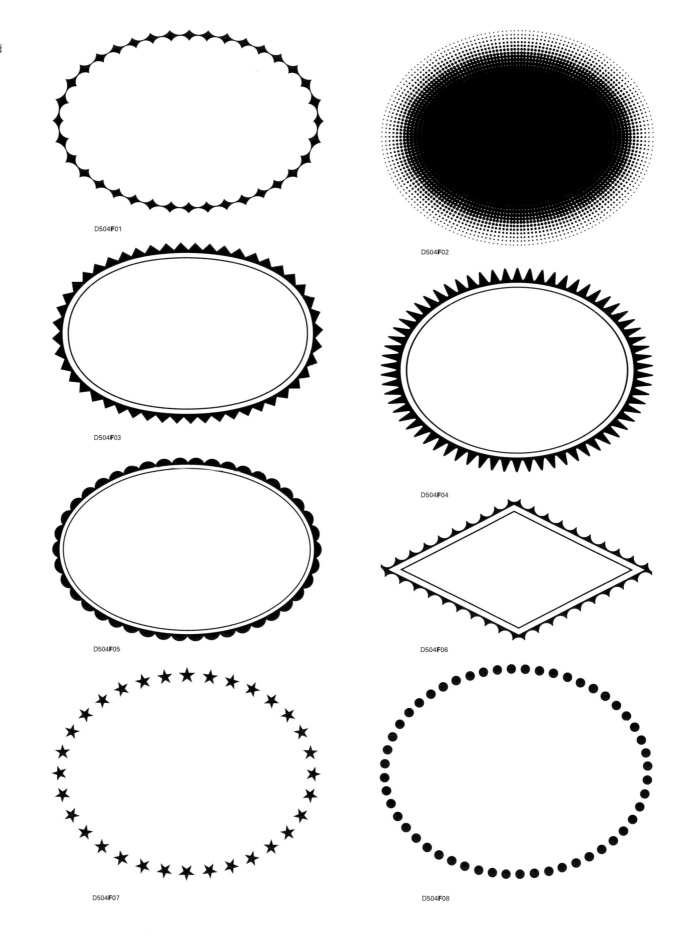

D504**F**01

D504**F**02

D504**F**03

D504F04

D504**F**05

D504F06

D504**F**07

D504F08

Seals
continued

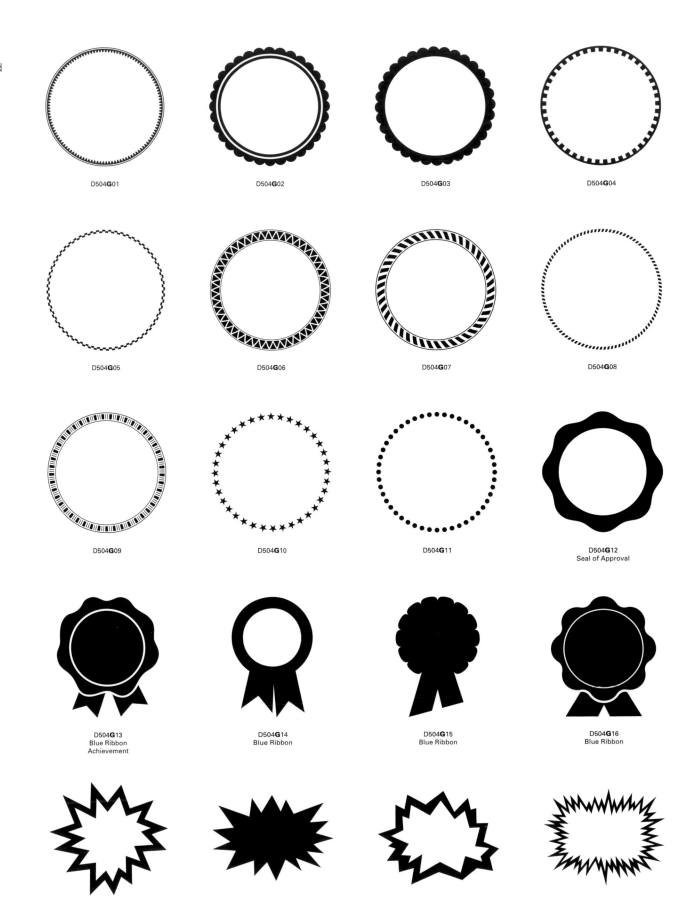

D504**G**01

D504**G**02

D504**G**03

D504**G**04

D504**G**05

D504**G**06

D504**G**07

D504**G**08

D504**G**09

D504**G**10

D504**G**11

D504**G**12
Seal of Approval

D504**G**13
Blue Ribbon
Achievement

D504**G**14
Blue Ribbon

D504**G**15
Blue Ribbon

D504**G**16
Blue Ribbon

Bursts

D504**G**17

D504**G**18

D504**G**19

D504**G**20

Bursts
continued

D504**H**01

D504**H**02

D504**H**03

D504**H**04

D504**H**05

D504**H**06

D504**H**07

D504**H**08

D504**H**09

D504**H**10

Fireworks

D504**H**11

D504**H**12

D504**H**13

D504**H**14

Banners

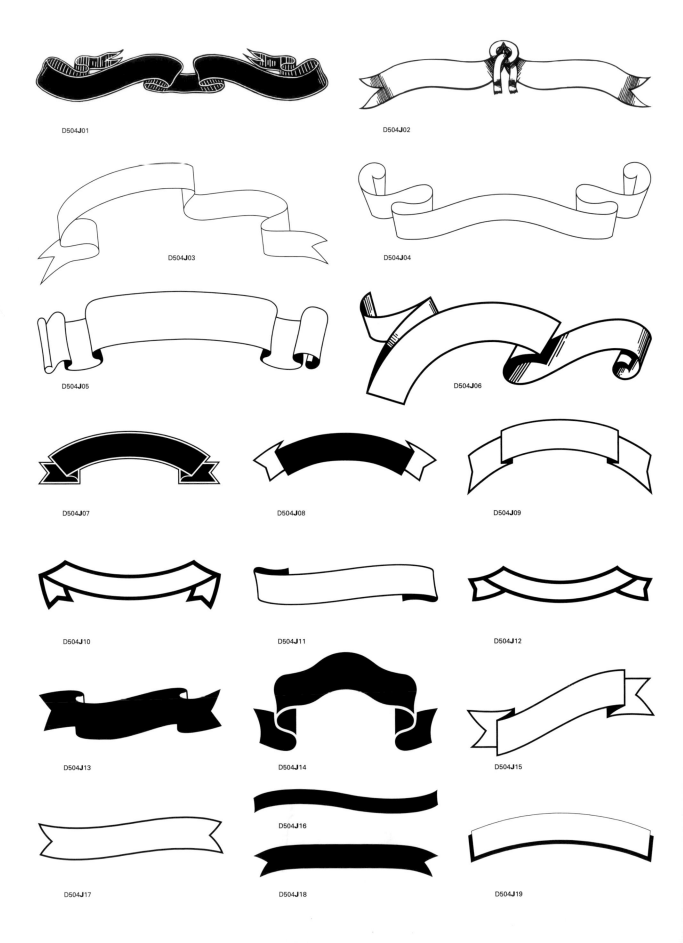

D504J01

D504J02

D504J03

D504J04

D504J05

D504J06

D504J07

D504J08

D504J09

D504J10

D504J11

D504J12

D504J13

D504J14

D504J15

D504J16

D504J17

D504J18

D504J19

Banners
continued

Flags
Pendants

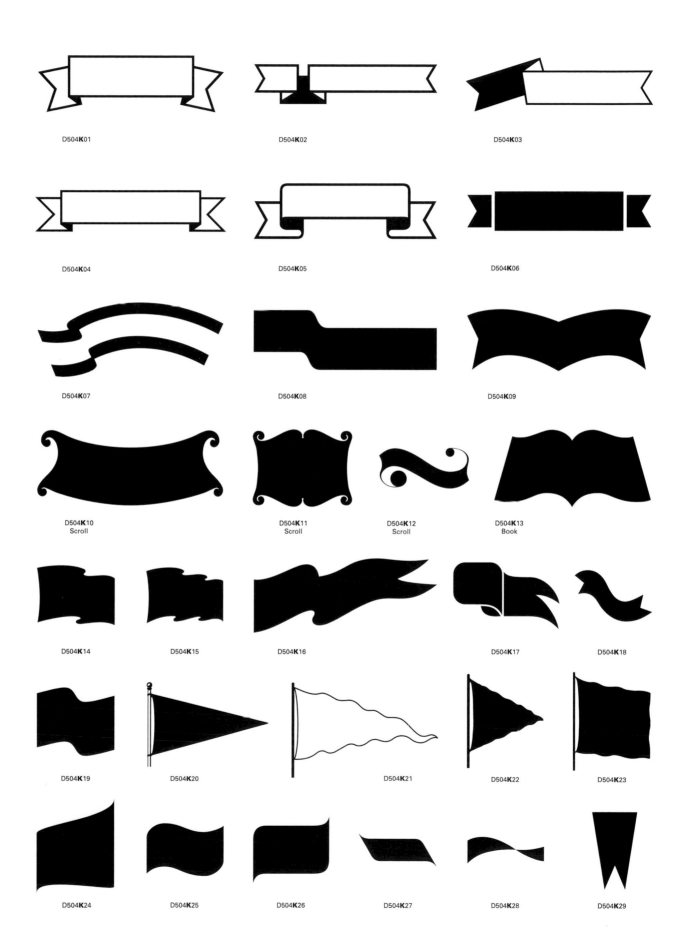

D504**K**01

D504**K**02

D504**K**03

D504**K**04

D504**K**05

D504**K**06

D504**K**07

D504**K**08

D504**K**09

D504**K**10
Scroll

D504**K**11
Scroll

D504**K**12
Scroll

D504**K**13
Book

D504**K**14

D504**K**15

D504**K**16

D504**K**17

D504**K**18

D504**K**19

D504**K**20

D504**K**21

D504**K**22

D504**K**23

D504**K**24

D504**K**25

D504**K**26

D504**K**27

D504**K**28

D504**K**29

Cartouches
Tablets

D504L01

D504L02

D504L03

D504L04

D504L05

D504L06

D504L07

D504L08

D504L09

D504L10

D504L11

D504L12

D504L13

D504L14

D504L15

D504L16

D504L17

D504L18

D504L19

D504L20

D504L21

D504L22

D504L23

D504L24

D504L25

D504L26

D504L27

D504L28

D504L29

D504L30
Ten Commandments

D504L31

D504L32

D504L33

D504L34

Cartouches
Tablets
continued

D504**M**01

D504**M**02

D504**M**03

D504**M**04

D504**M**05

D504**M**06

D504**M**07

D504**M**08

D504**M**09

D504**M**10

D504**M**11

D504**M**12

D504**M**13

D504**M**14

D504**M**15

D504**M**16

D504**M**17
Spanish Tiles

D504**M**18

D504**M**19

D504**M**20

D504**M**21

D504**M**22

D504**M**23

D504**M**24

D504**M**25

D504**M**26

D504**M**27

D504**M**28

D504**M**29

D504**M**30

D504**M**31

D504**M**32

D504**M**33

D504**M**34

D504**M**35

Cartouches
Tablets
continued

D504N01   D504N02   D504N03   D504N04   D504N05   D504N06

D504N07   D504N08   D504N09   D504N10   D504N11   D504N12

D504N13   D504N14   D504N15   D504N16   D504N17   D504N18

D504N19   D504N20   D504N21   D504N22   D504N23

D504N24   D504N25   D504N26   D504N27   D504N28   D504N29

D504N30   D504N31   D504N32   D504N33   D504N34

D504N35   D504N36   D504N37   D504N38   D504N39   D504N40

Cartouches
Tablets
continued
- Hanging Signs

D504**P**01

D504**P**02

D504**P**03

D504**P**04
Trumpet
Announcement

D504**P**05

D504**P**06

D504**P**07

D504**P**08

D504**P**09

D504**P**10

Cartouches
Tablets
continued

D504**S**01

D504**S**02

D504**S**03

D504**S**04

D504**S**05

D504**S**06

D504**S**07

D504**S**08

D504**S**09

D504**S**10

D504**S**11

D504**S**12

D504**S**13

D504**S**14

D504**S**15

D504**S**16

D504**S**17

D504**S**18

D504**S**19

D504**S**20

D504**S**21

D504**S**22

Cartouches
Tablets
continued

TV Screens

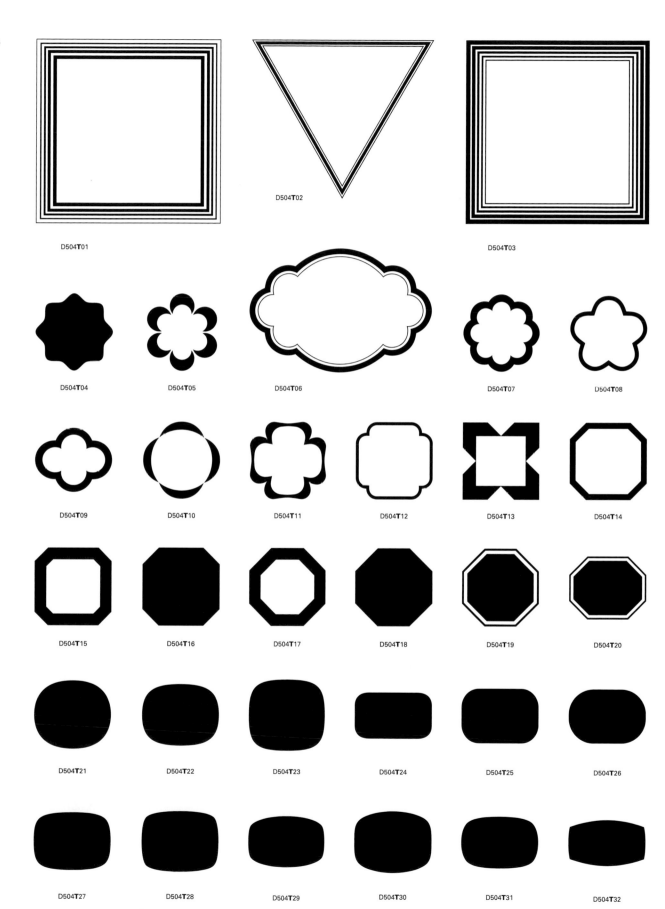

D504T01   D504T02   D504T03

D504T04   D504T05   D504T06   D504T07   D504T08

D504T09   D504T10   D504T11   D504T12   D504T13   D504T14

D504T15   D504T16   D504T17   D504T18   D504T19   D504T20

D504T21   D504T22   D504T23   D504T24   D504T25   D504T26

D504T27   D504T28   D504T29   D504T30   D504T31   D504T32

Blurbs

Bulb Shapes

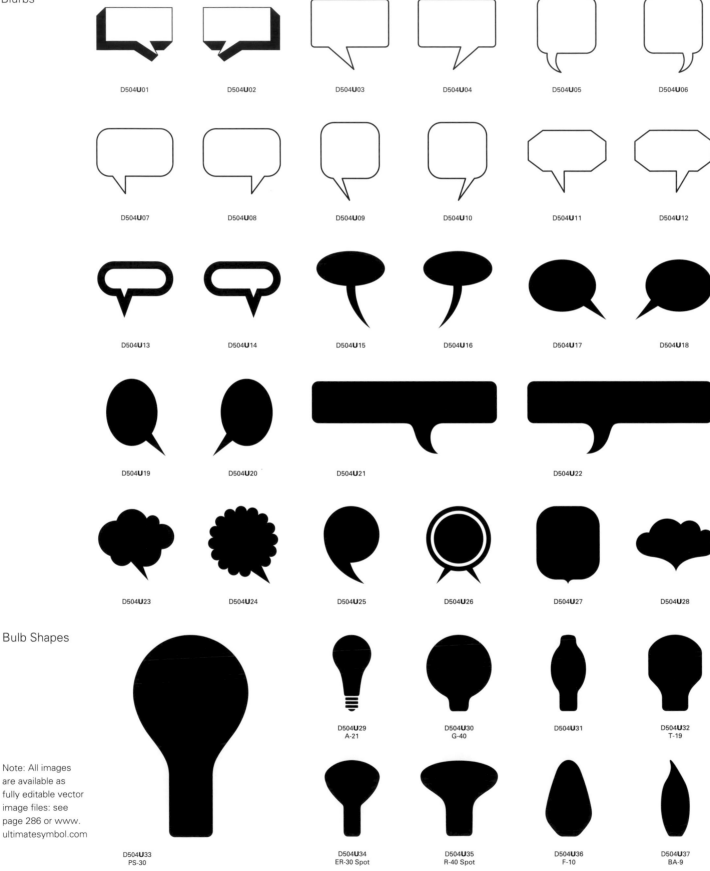

D504**U**01   D504**U**02   D504**U**03   D504**U**04   D504**U**05   D504**U**06

D504**U**07   D504**U**08   D504**U**09   D504**U**10   D504**U**11   D504**U**12

D504**U**13   D504**U**14   D504**U**15   D504**U**16   D504**U**17   D504**U**18

D504**U**19   D504**U**20   D504**U**21   D504**U**22

D504**U**23   D504**U**24   D504**U**25   D504**U**26   D504**U**27   D504**U**28

Note: All images
are available as
fully editable vector
image files: see
page 286 or www.
ultimatesymbol.com

D504**U**33
PS-30

D504**U**29
A-21

D504**U**30
G-40

D504**U**31

D504**U**32
T-19

D504**U**34
ER-30 Spot

D504**U**35
R-40 Spot

D504**U**36
F-10

D504**U**37
BA-9

Bell Shapes

D504**V**01   D504**V**02   D504**V**03   D504**V**04   D504**V**05   D504**V**06

D504**V**07   D504**V**08   D504**V**09   D504**V**10   D504**V**11   D504**V**12

Check Marks

D504**V**13   D504**V**14   D504**V**15   D504**V**16   D504**V**17   D504**V**18

D504**V**19   D504**V**20   D504**V**21   D504**V**22   D504**V**23   D504**V**24

D504**V**25   D504**V**26   D504**V**27   D504**V**28   D504**V**33

D504**V**29   D504**V**30   D504**V**31   D504**V**32
              Crisscross
              Censorship

Chevrons

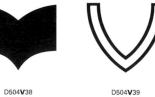

D504**V**34   D504**V**35   D504**V**36   D504**V**37   D504**V**38   D504**V**39

5

Radial

D505**A**01

D505**A**02

D505**A**03

D505**A**04

D505**A**05

D505**A**06

D505**A**07

D505**A**08

D505**A**09

D505**A**10

D505**A**11

D505**A**12

D505**A**13

D505**A**14

D505**A**15

D505**A**16

D505**A**17

D505**A**18

D505**A**19

D505**A**20

D505**A**21

D505**A**22

D505**A**23

D505**A**24

D505**A**25

D505**A**26

D505**A**27

Radial
continued

D505**B**01 D505**B**02 D505**B**03 D505**B**04 D505**B**05

D505**B**06 D505**B**07 D505**B**08

D505**B**09 D505**B**10 D505**B**11 D505**B**12

D505**B**13 D505**B**14 D505**B**15 D505**B**16 D505**B**17

Early American
- Pennsylvania
  Dutch
- Quilt

D505**B**18 D505**B**19 D505**B**20 D505**B**21 D505**B**22

D505**B**23 D505**B**24 D505**B**25 D505**B**26
D505**B**27

Early American
continued
- Pennsylvania
  Dutch
- Quilt

D505**C**02

D505**C**03

D505**C**04

D505**C**05

D505**C**01

D505**C**06

D505**C**07

D505**C**08

D505**C**09

D505**C**10

D505**C**11

D505**C**12

D505**C**13

D505**C**14

D505**C**15

D505**C**16

D505**C**17

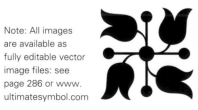

D505**C**18

D505**C**19

D505**C**20

D505**C**21

D505**C**22

Early American
continued
- Pennsylvania
  Dutch
- Quilt

D505**D**01   D505**D**02   D505**D**03   D505**D**04   D505**D**05

D505**D**06   D505**D**07   D505**D**08   D505**D**09   D505**D**10

D505**D**11   D505**D**12   D505**D**13   D505**D**14   D505**D**15

D505**D**16   D505**D**17   D505**D**18   D505**D**19   D505**D**20

D505**D**21   D505**D**22   D505**D**23   D505**D**24   D505**D**25

D505**D**26   D505**D**27   D505**D**28   D505**D**29   D505**D**30

Early American
continued
- Pennsylvania
  Dutch
- Quilt

D505E01

D505E02

D505E03

D505E04

D505E05

D505E06

D505E07

D505E08

D505E09

D505E10

D505E11

D505E12

D505E13

D505E14

D505E15

-Square

D505E16

D505E17

D505E18

D505E19

D505E20

D505E21

D505E22

D505E23

D505E24

D505E25

Early American
continued
- Pennsylvania
  Dutch
- Quilt
- Square

D505F01

D505F02

D505F03

D505F04

D505F05

D505F06

D505F07

D505F08

D505F09

D505F10

D505F11

D505F12

D505F13

D505F14

D505F15

D505F16

D505F17

D505F18

D505F19

D505F20

D505F21

D505F22

D505F23

D505F24

D505F25

D505F26

D505F27

General

D505**G**01   D505**G**02   D505**G**03   D505**G**04

D505**G**05   D505**G**06   D505**G**07

D505**G**08   D505**G**09   D505**G**10

D505**G**11   D505**G**12   D505**G**13   D505**G**14   D505**G**15

D505**G**16   D505**G**17   D505**G**18   D505**G**19

D505**G**20   D505**G**21   D505**G**22   D505**G**23   D505**G**24

General
continued

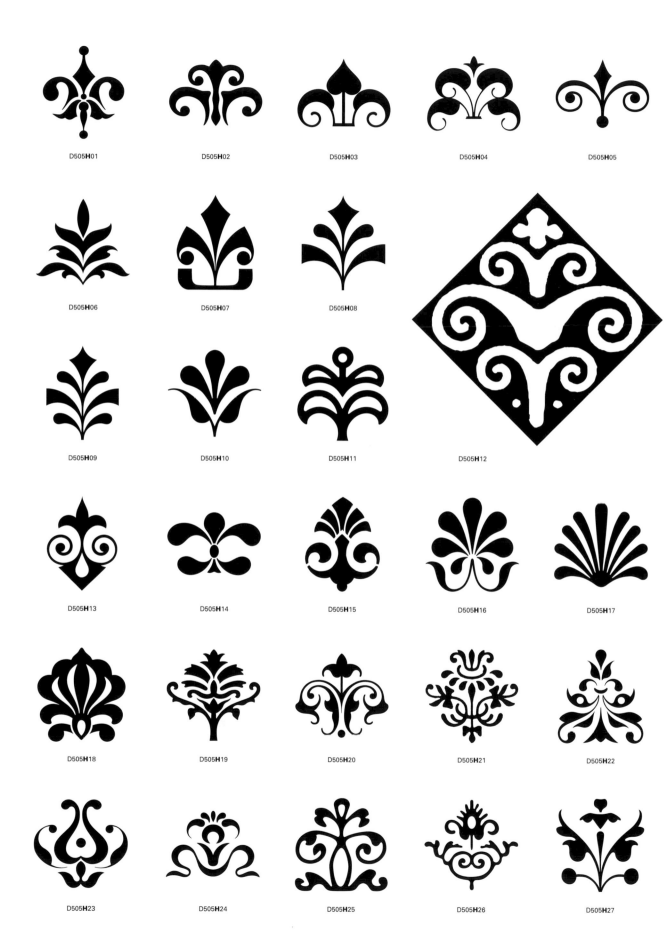

D505H01

D505H02

D505H03

D505H04

D505H05

D505H06

D505H07

D505H08

D505H09

D505H10

D505H11

D505H12

D505H13

D505H14

D505H15

D505H16

D505H17

D505H18

D505H19

D505H20

D505H21

D505H22

D505H23

D505H24

D505H25

D505H26

D505H27

General
continued

D505J01   D505J02   D505J03   D505J04   D505J05

D505J06   D505J07   D505J08

D505J09   D505J10   D505J11   D505J12

D505J13   D505J14   D505J15   D505J16   D505J17

D505J18   D505J19   D505J20   D505J21   D505J22

D505J23   D505J24   D505J25   D505J26   D505J27

General
continued

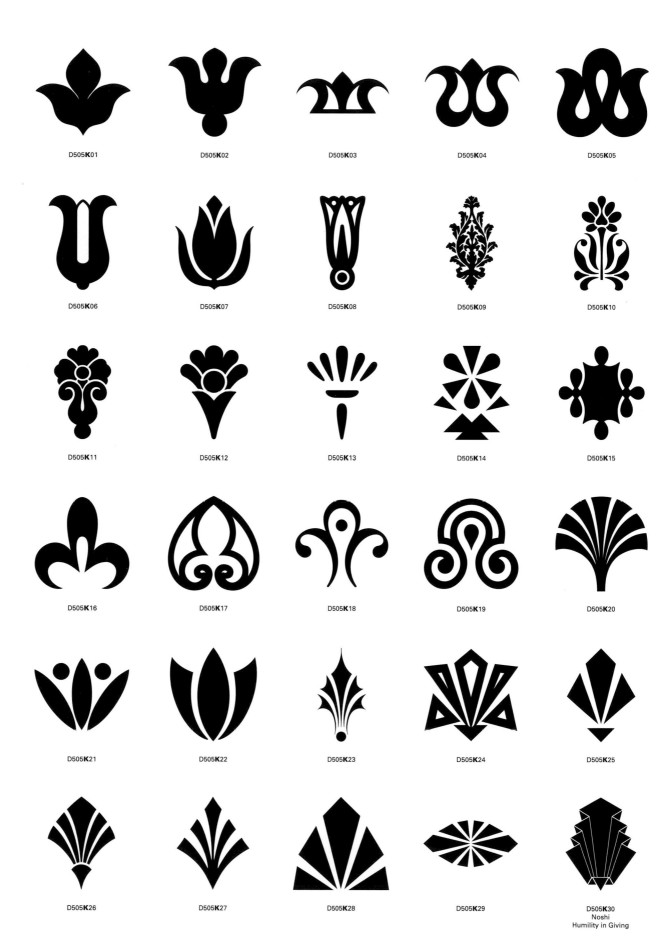

D505**K**01

D505**K**02

D505**K**03

D505**K**04

D505**K**05

D505**K**06

D505**K**07

D505**K**08

D505**K**09

D505**K**10

D505**K**11

D505**K**12

D505**K**13

D505**K**14

D505**K**15

D505**K**16

D505**K**17

D505**K**18

D505**K**19

D505**K**20

D505**K**21

D505**K**22

D505**K**23

D505**K**24

D505**K**25

D505**K**26

D505**K**27

D505**K**28

D505**K**29

D505**K**30
Noshi
Humility in Giving

General
continued

D505L01

D505L02

D505L03

D505L04

D505L05

D505L06

D505L07

D505L08

D505L09

D505L10

D505L11

D505L12

D505L13

D505L14

D505L15

D505L16

D505L17

D505L18

D505L19

D505L20

D505L21

D505L22

D505L23

D505L24

General
continued

D505M01   D505M02   D505M03   D505M04   D505M05

D505M06   D505M07   D505M08   D505M09   D505M10

D505M11   D505M12   D505M13   D505M14   D505M15

D505M16   D505M17   D505M18   D505M19   D505M20

D505M21   D505M22   D505M23   D505M24   D505M25

D505M26   D505M27   D505M28   D505M29   D505M30

General
- Acorns

D505N01

D505N02

D505N03

D505N04

D505N05
Acorn
Longevity

D505N06

D505N07

D505N08

D505N09

D505N10

D505N11

D505N12

D505N13

D505N14

D505N15

- Hearts

D505N16

D505N17

D505N18

D505N19

D505N20

D505N21

D505N22

- Leaves

D505P01

D505P02

D505P03

D505P04

D505P05

D505P06

D505P07

D505P08

D505P09

D505P10

D505P11

D505P12

D505P13

D505P14

D505P15

D505P16

- Musical

D505P17

D505P18

D505P19

D505P20

D505P21
F-holes

D505P22
G-clef

D505P23
Horn
Bugle

D505P24
Organ Pipes

D505P25
Sistrum of Isis
Conscience

D505P26
Lyre

- Musical
  continued

D505**Q**01
Lyre

D505**Q**02
Lyre

D505**Q**03
Lyre

D505**Q**04

D505**Q**05

D505**Q**06

D505**Q**07

D505**Q**08

D505**Q**09

D505**Q**10

- Fleur de Lis

D505**Q**14
Fleur de Lis
The Flower of Light
Life and Power

D505**Q**11

D505**Q**12

D505**Q**13

D505**Q**15

D505**Q**16

D505**Q**17

D505**Q**18

D505**Q**19

D505**Q**20

D505**Q**21

D505**Q**22

Note: All images
are available as
fully editable vector
image files: see
page 286 or www.
ultimatesymbol.com

D505**Q**23

D505**Q**24

D505**Q**25

D505**Q**26

D505**Q**27

- Fleur de Lis
continued

D505R01

D505R02

D505R03

D505R04

D505R05

D505R06

D505R07

D505R08

D505R09

D505R10

General

D505R11
Lion
Courage

D505R12
Lion

D505R13
Dragon
Vigilance

D505R14
Celix and Serpent
Hygiene

D505R15
Hourglass

D505R16
Vase

D505R17

D505R18
Top

D505R19

D505R20

D505R21

D505R22

D505R23

D505R24

D505R25

D505R26

D505R27

6

Pointers
- Hands
 (woodcut)

D506**A**01

D506**A**02

D506**A**03

D506**A**04

D506**A**05

D506**A**06

D506**A**07

D506**A**08

D506**A**09

D506**A**10

D506**A**11

D506**A**12

D506**A**13

D506**A**14

D506**A**15

D506**A**16

D506**A**17

D506**A**18

D506**A**19

D506**A**20

Pointers
- Hands
  (woodcut)
  continued

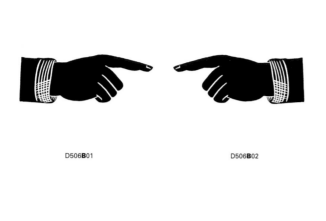

D506**B**01   D506**B**02   D506**B**03   D506**B**04

D506**B**05   D506**B**06   D506**B**07   D506**B**08

D506**B**09   D506**B**10   D506**B**11   D506**B**12

D506**B**13   D506**B**14   D506**B**15   D506**B**16

D506**B**17   D506**B**18   D506**B**19   D506**B**20

Pointers
- Hands
  (general)
  continued

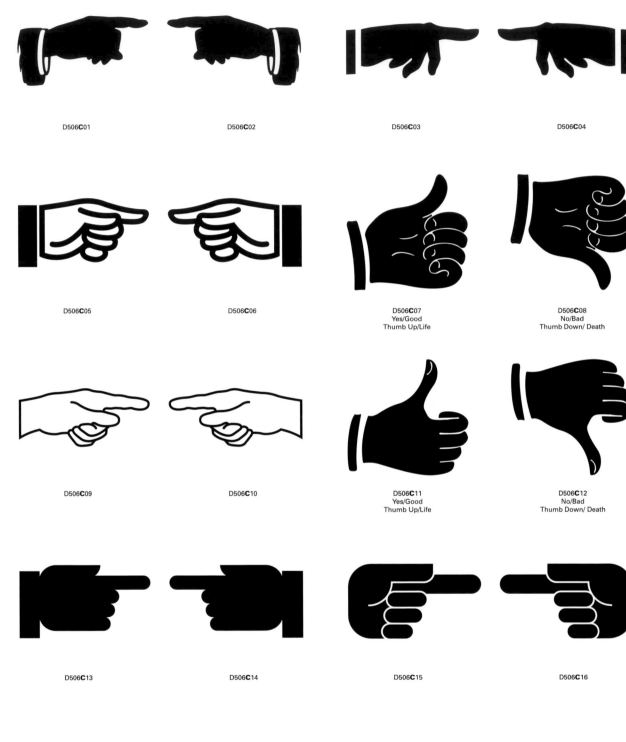

D506**C**01

D506**C**02

D506**C**03

D506**C**04

D506**C**05

D506**C**06

D506**C**07
Yes/Good
Thumb Up/Life

D506**C**08
No/Bad
Thumb Down/ Death

D506**C**09

D506**C**10

D506**C**11
Yes/Good
Thumb Up/Life

D506**C**12
No/Bad
Thumb Down/ Death

D506**C**13

D506**C**14

D506**C**15

D506**C**16

Note: All images
are available as
fully editable vector
image files: see
page 286 or www.
ultimatesymbol.com

D506**C**17

D506**C**18

D506**C**19

D506**C**20

Pointers
- Hands
  (general)
  continued

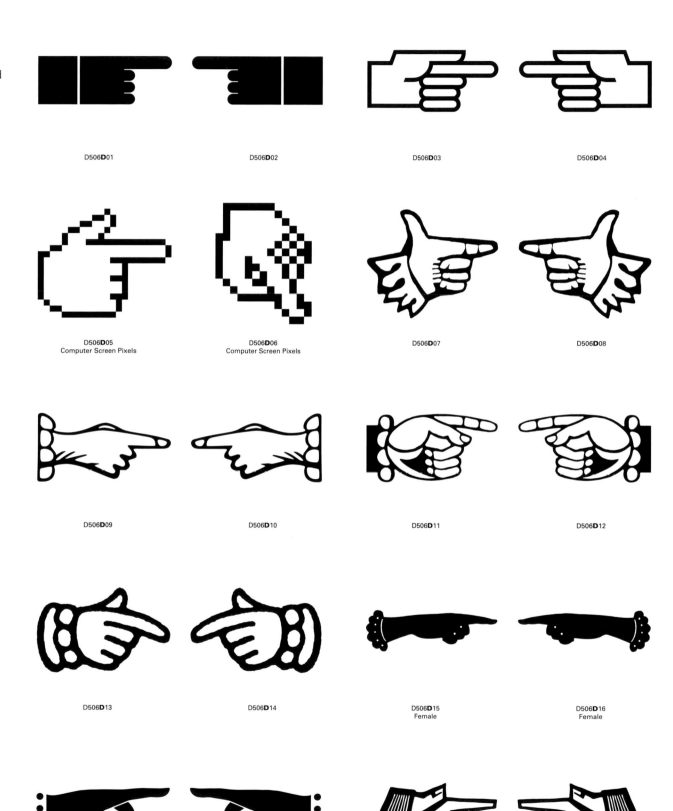

D506**D**01

D506**D**02

D506**D**03

D506**D**04

D506**D**05
Computer Screen Pixels

D506**D**06
Computer Screen Pixels

D506**D**07

D506**D**08

D506**D**09

D506**D**10

D506**D**11

D506**D**12

D506**D**13

D506**D**14

D506**D**15
Female

D506**D**16
Female

D506**D**17
Female

D506**D**18
Female

D506**D**19

D506**D**20

Pointers
- Hands
  (general)
  continued

- Clock Hands

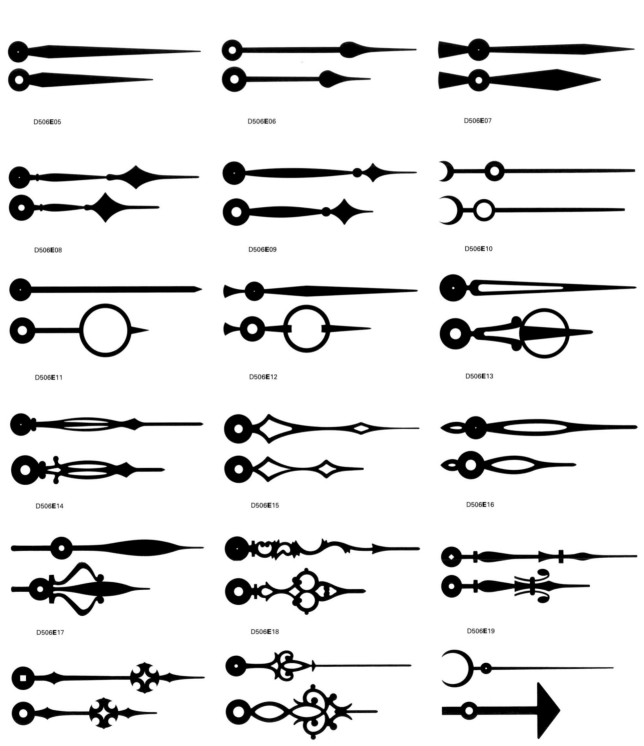

D506E01

D506E02

D506E03

D506E04

D506E05

D506E06

D506E07

D506E08

D506E09

D506E10

D506E11

D506E12

D506E13

D506E14

D506E15

D506E16

D506E17

D506E18

D506E19

D506E20

D506E21

D506E22

Pointers
continued
- Weather Vanes

D506F01
Bird
Rooster

D506F02
Bird
Rooster

D506F03
Bird
Rooster

D506F04
Bird

D506F05
Bird
Pheasant

D506F06
Bird
Eagle

D506F07
Bird
Eagle

D506F08
Bird
Eagle

D506F09
Horse

D506F10
Horse

D506F11
Horse

D506F12
Horse and Rider

D506F13
Horse and Carriage

D506F14
Horse and Carriage

D506F15
Horse and Carriage

D506F16
Dog

D506F17
Deer
Stag

D506F18
Deer
Stag

D506F19
Cow

D506F20
Fox

Pointers
- Weather Vanes
  continued

D506**G**01
Boat
Sailing Ship

D506**G**02
Boat
Sailing Ship

D506**G**03
Whale
Sperm

D506**G**04
Fish

D506**G**05
Serpent
Whale

D506**G**06
Angel

D506**G**07
Angel
Gabriel

D506**G**08
Angel
Gabriel

D506**G**09
Cupid
Love

D506**G**10
Woman
Herald

D506**G**11
Woman
Liberty

D506**G**12
Woman
Statue of Liberty

D506**G**13
Indian
Archer

D506**G**14
Indian
Archer

D506**G**15
Archer

D506**G**16
Weather Vane
Inconstancy

D506**G**17

D506**G**18

D506**G**19

D506**G**20

Pointers
continued
- Animals

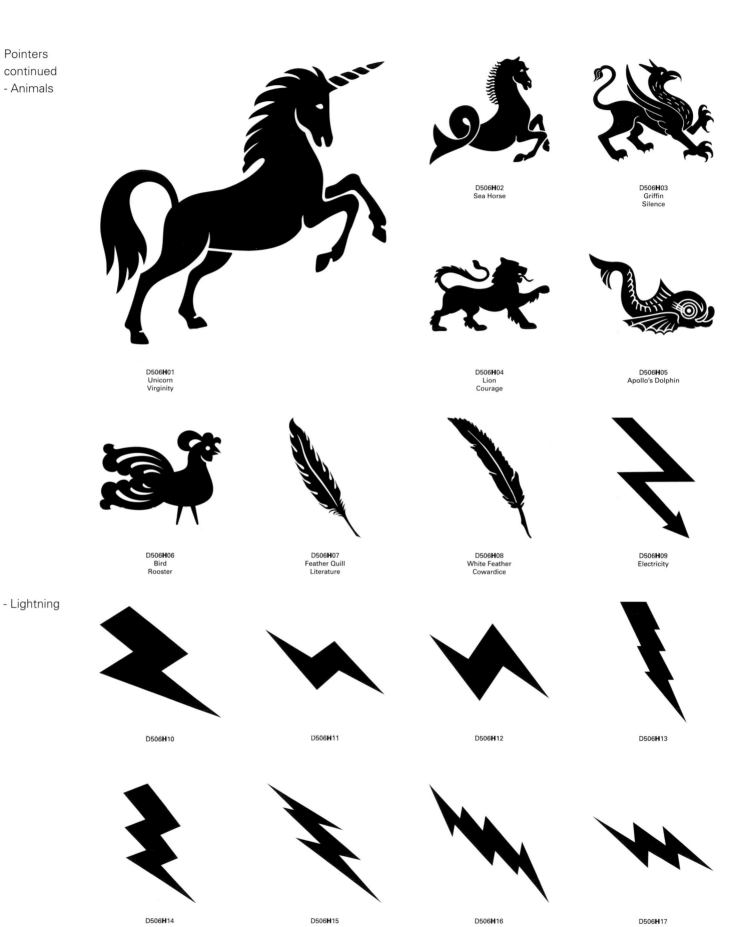

D506H02
Sea Horse

D506H03
Griffin
Silence

D506H01
Unicorn
Virginity

D506H04
Lion
Courage

D506H05
Apollo's Dolphin

D506H06
Bird
Rooster

D506H07
Feather Quill
Literature

D506H08
White Feather
Cowardice

D506H09
Electricity

- Lightning

D506H10

D506H11

D506H12

D506H13

D506H14

D506H15

D506H16

D506H17

Arrows
- International

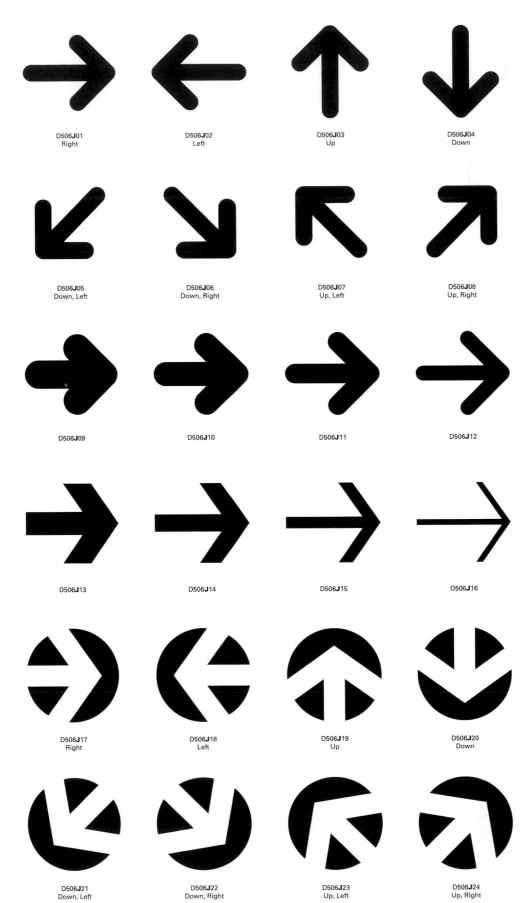

D506J01
Right

D506J02
Left

D506J03
Up

D506J04
Down

D506J05
Down, Left

D506J06
Down, Right

D506J07
Up, Left

D506J08
Up, Right

D506J09

D506J10

D506J11

D506J12

D506J13

D506J14

D506J15

D506J16

D506J17
Right

D506J18
Left

D506J19
Up

D506J20
Down

D506J21
Down, Left

D506J22
Down, Right

D506J23
Up, Left

D506J24
Up, Right

Arrows
- International
  continued

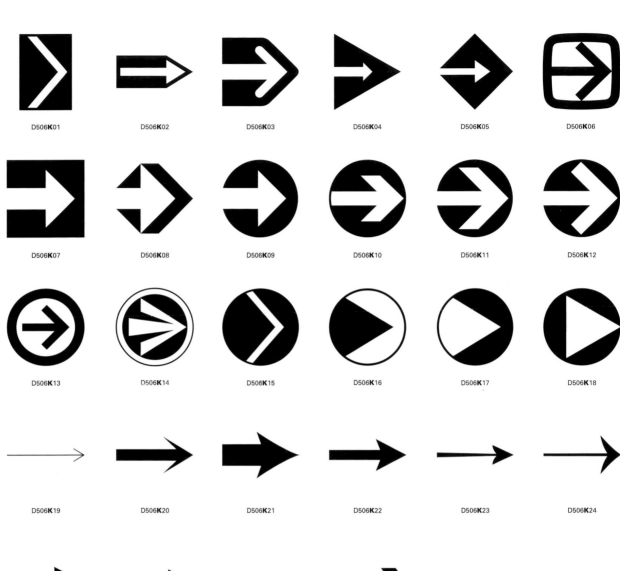

D506**K**01   D506**K**02   D506**K**03   D506**K**04   D506**K**05   D506**K**06

D506**K**07   D506**K**08   D506**K**09   D506**K**10   D506**K**11   D506**K**12

D506**K**13   D506**K**14   D506**K**15   D506**K**16   D506**K**17   D506**K**18

- General

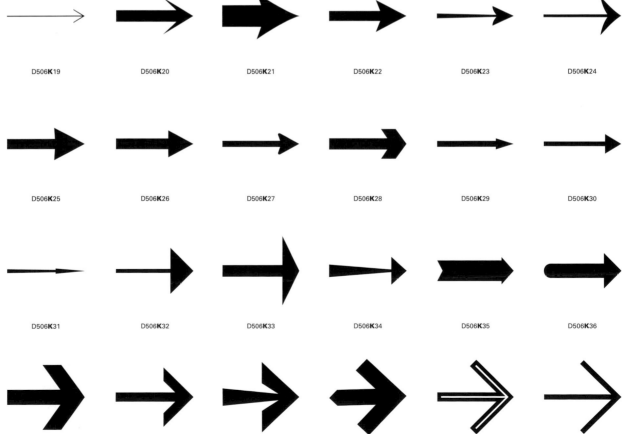

D506**K**19   D506**K**20   D506**K**21   D506**K**22   D506**K**23   D506**K**24

D506**K**25   D506**K**26   D506**K**27   D506**K**28   D506**K**29   D506**K**30

D506**K**31   D506**K**32   D506**K**33   D506**K**34   D506**K**35   D506**K**36

D506**K**37   D506**K**38   D506**K**39   D506**K**40   D506**K**41   D506**K**42

Arrows
- General
continued

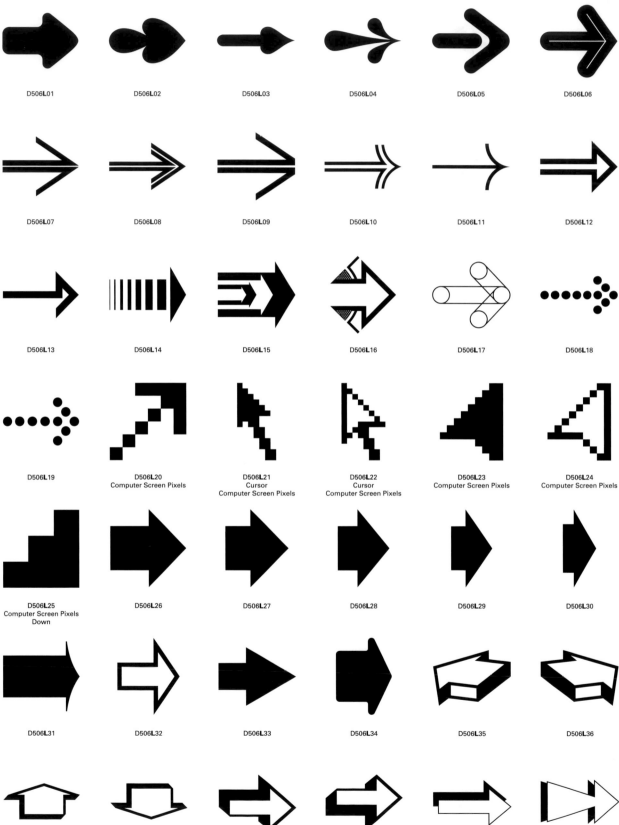

D506L01   D506L02   D506L03   D506L04   D506L05   D506L06

D506L07   D506L08   D506L09   D506L10   D506L11   D506L12

D506L13   D506L14   D506L15   D506L16   D506L17   D506L18

D506L19   D506L20
Computer Screen Pixels   D506L21
Cursor
Computer Screen Pixels   D506L22
Cursor
Computer Screen Pixels   D506L23
Computer Screen Pixels   D506L24
Computer Screen Pixels

D506L25
Computer Screen Pixels
Down   D506L26   D506L27   D506L28   D506L29   D506L30

D506L31   D506L32   D506L33   D506L34   D506L35   D506L36

D506L37   D506L38   D506L39   D506L40   D506L41   D506L42

Arrows
- General
continued

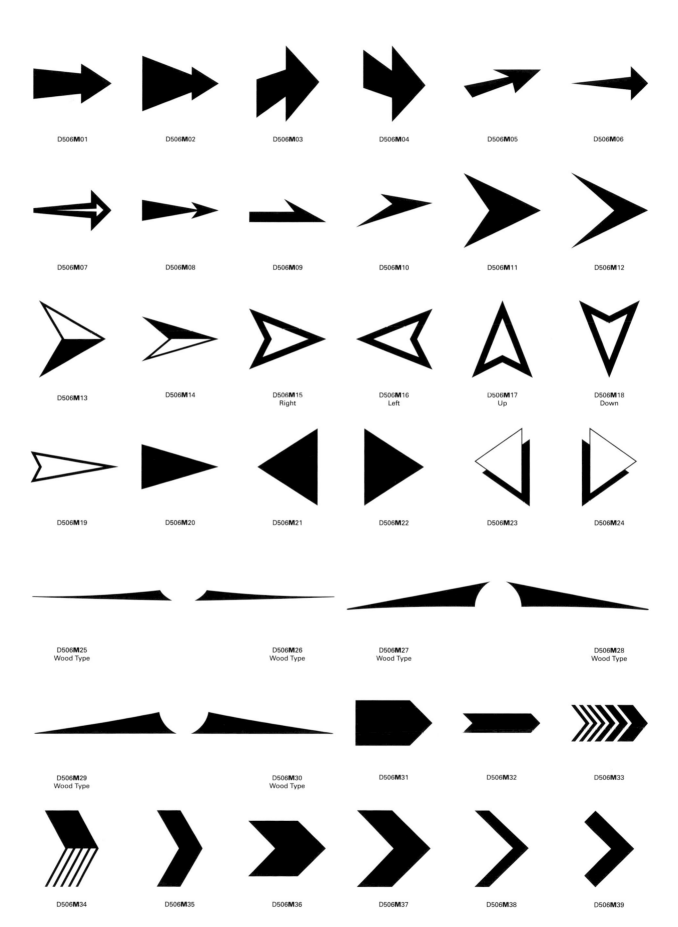

D506M01

D506M02

D506M03

D506M04

D506M05

D506M06

D506M07

D506M08

D506M09

D506M10

D506M11

D506M12

D506M13

D506M14

D506M15
Right

D506M16
Left

D506M17
Up

D506M18
Down

D506M19

D506M20

D506M21

D506M22

D506M23

D506M24

D506M25
Wood Type

D506M26
Wood Type

D506M27
Wood Type

D506M28
Wood Type

D506M29
Wood Type

D506M30
Wood Type

D506M31

D506M32

D506M33

D506M34

D506M35

D506M36

D506M37

D506M38

D506M39

Arrows
- Multi-directional

- Curved

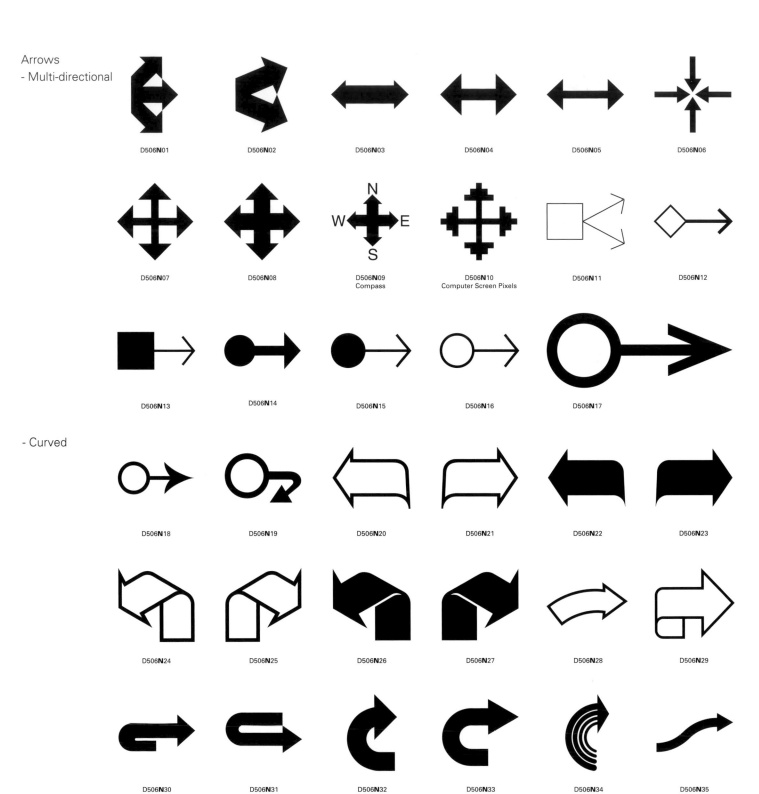

D506N01   D506N02   D506N03   D506N04   D506N05   D506N06

D506N07   D506N08   D506N09   D506N10   D506N11   D506N12
                      Compass   Computer Screen Pixels

D506N13   D506N14   D506N15   D506N16   D506N17

D506N18   D506N19   D506N20   D506N21   D506N22   D506N23

D506N24   D506N25   D506N26   D506N27   D506N28   D506N29

D506N30   D506N31   D506N32   D506N33   D506N34   D506N35

D506N36   D506N37   D506N38   D506N39   D506N40   D506N41

Arrows
- Curved
  continued

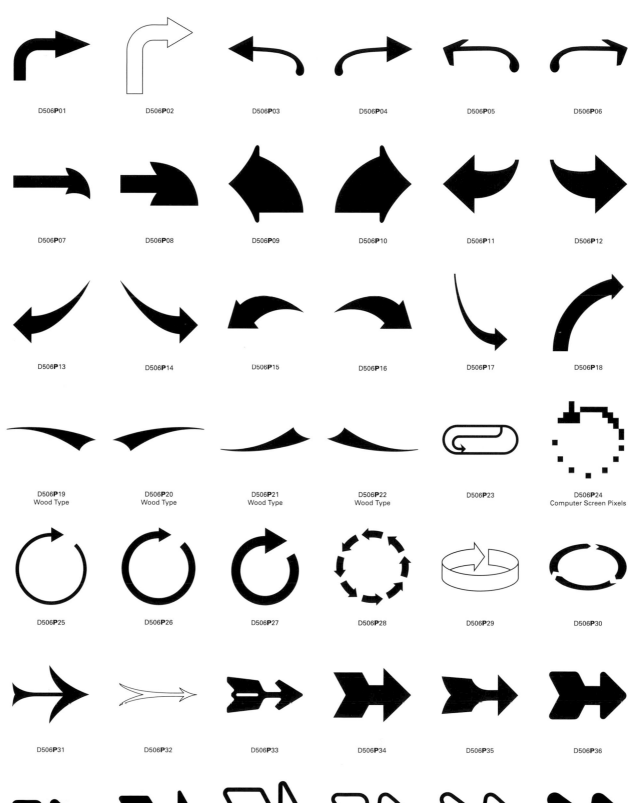

D506**P**01	D506**P**02	D506**P**03	D506**P**04	D506**P**05	D506**P**06
D506**P**07	D506**P**08	D506**P**09	D506**P**10	D506**P**11	D506**P**12
D506**P**13	D506**P**14	D506**P**15	D506**P**16	D506**P**17	D506**P**18
D506**P**19 Wood Type	D506**P**20 Wood Type	D506**P**21 Wood Type	D506**P**22 Wood Type	D506**P**23	D506**P**24 Computer Screen Pixels
D506**P**25	D506**P**26	D506**P**27	D506**P**28	D506**P**29	D506**P**30

- Tail

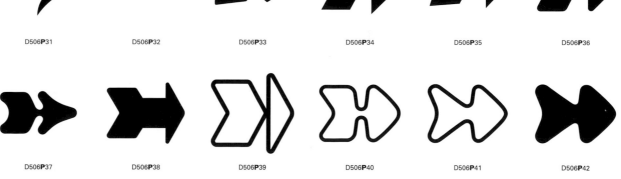

D506**P**31	D506**P**32	D506**P**33	D506**P**34	D506**P**35	D506**P**36
D506**P**37	D506**P**38	D506**P**39	D506**P**40	D506**P**41	D506**P**42

Arrows
- Tail
continued

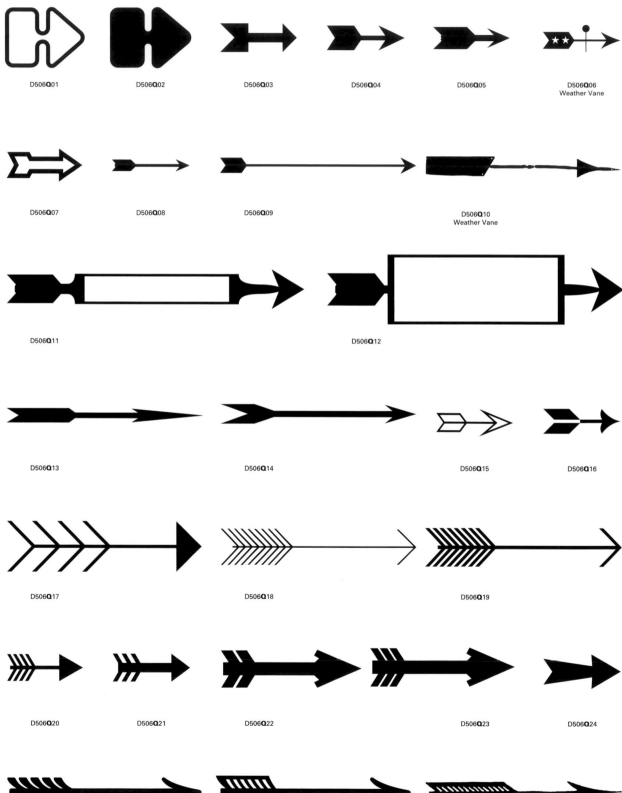

D506Q01

D506Q02

D506Q03

D506Q04

D506Q05

D506Q06
Weather Vane

D506Q07

D506Q08

D506Q09

D506Q10
Weather Vane

D506Q11

D506Q12

D506Q13

D506Q14

D506Q15

D506Q16

D506Q17

D506Q18

D506Q19

D506Q20

D506Q21

D506Q22

D506Q23

D506Q24

Note: All images
are available as
fully editable vector
image files: see
page 286 or www.
ultimatesymbol.com

D506Q25

D506Q26

D506Q27
Wood Type

Arrows
- Tail
  continued

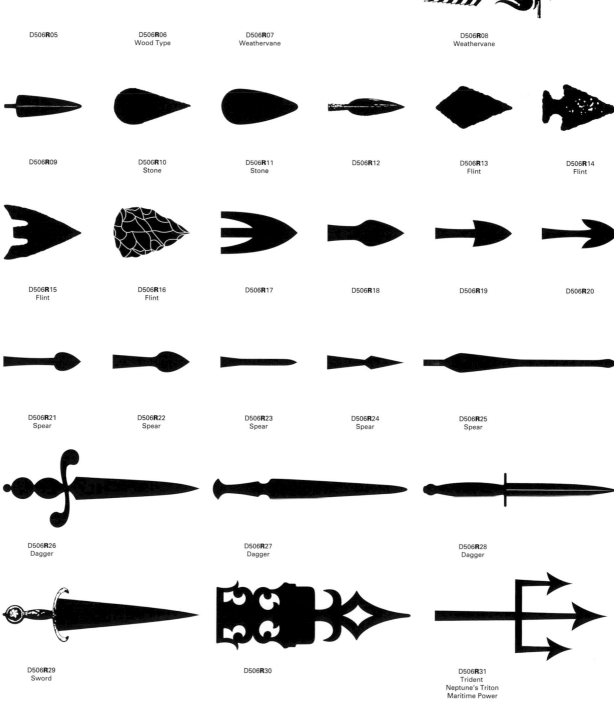

- Head
  (ancient)

D506**R**01

D506**R**02

D506**R**03
Wood Type

D506**R**04

D506**R**05

D506**R**06
Wood Type

D506**R**07
Weathervane

D506**R**08
Weathervane

D506**R**09

D506**R**10
Stone

D506**R**11
Stone

D506**R**12

D506**R**13
Flint

D506**R**14
Flint

D506**R**15
Flint

D506**R**16
Flint

D506**R**17

D506**R**18

D506**R**19

D506**R**20

D506**R**21
Spear

D506**R**22
Spear

D506**R**23
Spear

D506**R**24
Spear

D506**R**25
Spear

D506**R**26
Dagger

D506**R**27
Dagger

D506**R**28
Dagger

D506**R**29
Sword

D506**R**30

D506**R**31
Trident
Neptune's Triton
Maritime Power

7

Snowflakes

D507**A**01

D507**A**02

D507**A**03

D507**A**04

D507**A**05

D507**A**06

D507**A**07

D507**A**08

D507**A**09

D507**A**10

D507**A**11

D507**A**12

D507**A**13

D507**A**14

D507**A**15

D507**A**16

D507**A**17

D507**A**18

D507**A**19

D507**A**20

D507**A**21

D507**A**22

D507**A**23

D507**A**24

Snowflakes
continued

D507**B**01   D507**B**02   D507**B**03   D507**B**04   D507**B**05

D507**B**06   D507**B**07   D507**B**08

D507**B**09   D507**B**10   D507**B**11   D507**B**12

D507**B**13   D507**B**14   D507**B**15   D507**B**16   D507**B**17

D507**B**18   D507**B**19   D507**B**20

D507**B**21   D507**B**22   D507**B**23   D507**B**24

Targets
Concentric
Circles

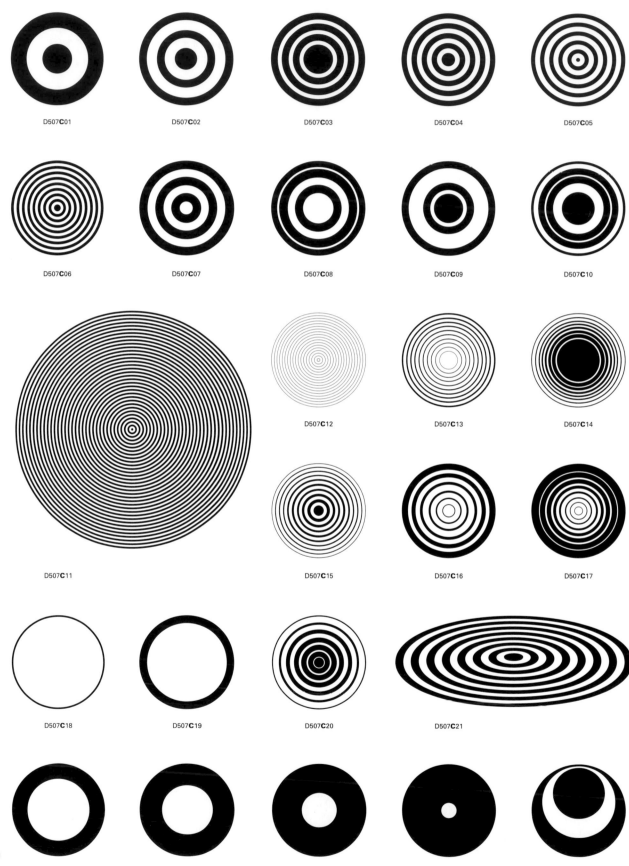

D507**C**01   D507**C**02   D507**C**03   D507**C**04   D507**C**05

D507**C**06   D507**C**07   D507**C**08   D507**C**09   D507**C**10

D507**C**11   D507**C**12   D507**C**13   D507**C**14

D507**C**15   D507**C**16   D507**C**17

D507**C**18   D507**C**19   D507**C**20   D507**C**21

Note: All images
are available as
fully editable vector
image files: see
page 286 or www.
ultimatesymbol.com

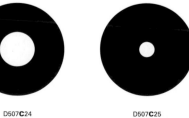

D507**C**22   D507**C**23   D507**C**24   D507**C**25   D507**C**26

Concentric
Circles
continued

Spirals

D507**D**01

D507**D**02

D507**D**03

D507**D**04

D507**D**05

D507**D**06

D507**D**07

D507**D**08

D507**D**09

D507**D**10

D507**D**11

D507**D**12

D507**D**13

D507**D**14

D507**D**15

D507**D**16

D507**D**17

D507**D**18

D507**D**19

D507**D**20

D507**D**21

D507**D**22

D507**D**23

D507**D**24

D507**D**25

D507**D**26

Whirls

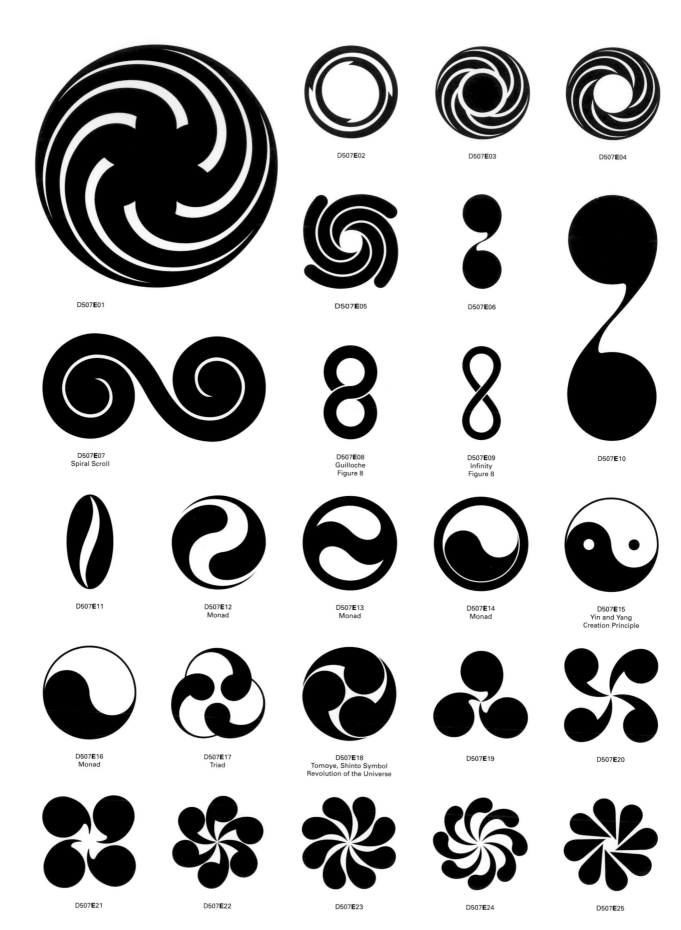

D507E02

D507E03

D507E04

D507E01

D507E05

D507E06

D507E07
Spiral Scroll

D507E08
Guilloche
Figure 8

D507E09
Infinity
Figure 8

D507E10

D507E11

D507E12
Monad

D507E13
Monad

D507E14
Monad

D507E15
Yin and Yang
Creation Principle

D507E16
Monad

D507E17
Triad

D507E18
Tomoye, Shinto Symbol
Revolution of the Universe

D507E19

D507E20

D507E21

D507E22

D507E23

D507E24

D507E25

Pinwheels

D507F01　　　　D507F02　　　　D507F03　　　　D507F04　　　　D507F05

D507F06　　　　D507F07　　　　D507F08　　　　D507F09　　　　D507F10

D507F11　　　　　　　D507F12

D507F13　　　　D507F14

D507F15　　　　D507F16　　　　D507F17　　　　D507F18　　　　D507F19

D507F20　　　　D507F21　　　　D507F22　　　　D507F23　　　　D507F24

Pinwheels
continued

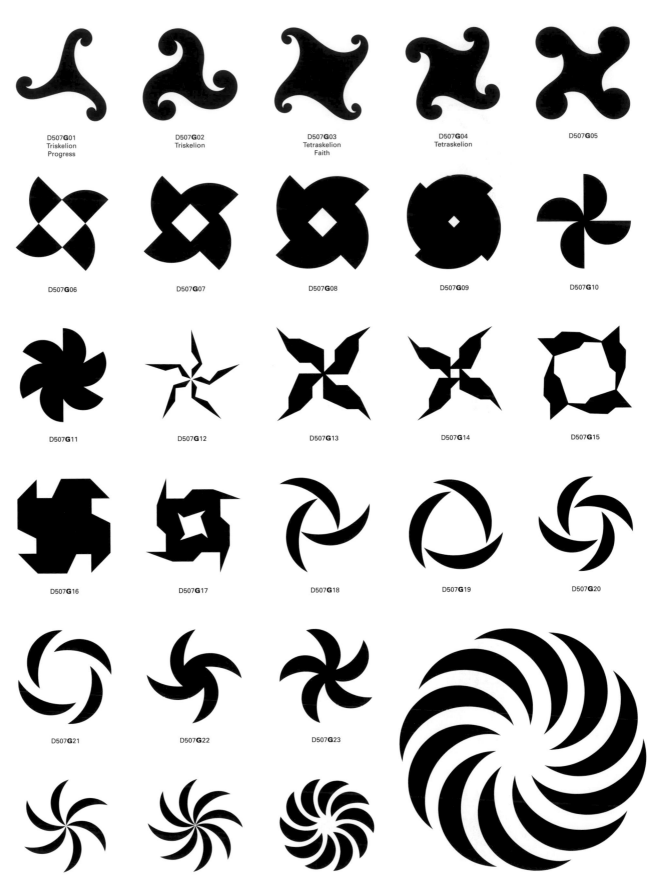

D507**G**01
Triskelion
Progress

D507**G**02
Triskelion

D507**G**03
Tetraskelion
Faith

D507**G**04
Tetraskelion

D507**G**05

D507**G**06

D507**G**07

D507**G**08

D507**G**09

D507**G**10

D507**G**11

D507**G**12

D507**G**13

D507**G**14

D507**G**15

D507**G**16

D507**G**17

D507**G**18

D507**G**19

D507**G**20

D507**G**21

D507**G**22

D507**G**23

D507**G**24

D507**G**25

D507**G**26

D507**G**27

Pinwheels
continued

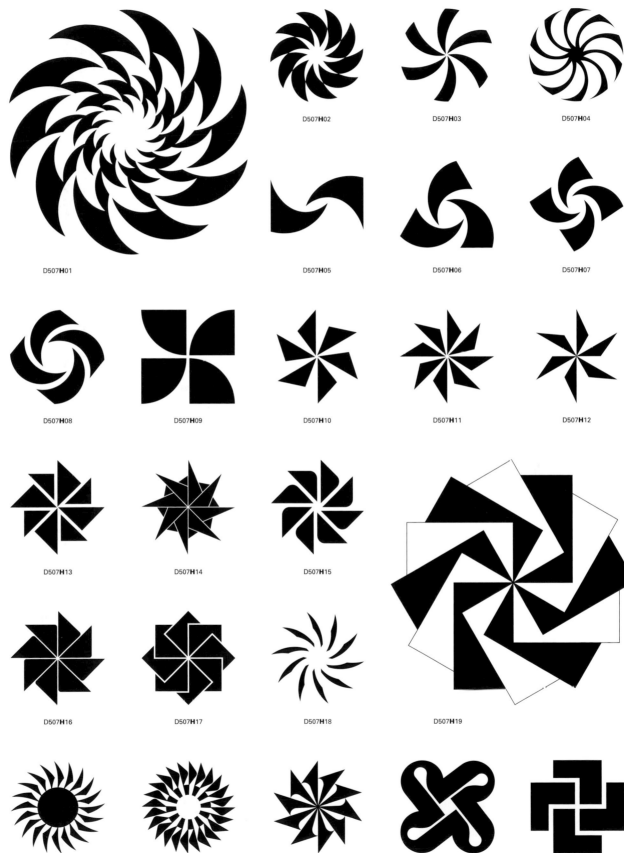

D507H01

D507H02

D507H03

D507H04

D507H05

D507H06

D507H07

D507H08

D507H09

D507H10

D507H11

D507H12

D507H13

D507H14

D507H15

D507H16

D507H17

D507H18

D507H19

D507H20

D507H21

D507H22

D507H23

D507H24

Rotors

D507J01

D507J02

D507J03

D507J04

D507J05

D507J06

D507J07

D507J08
Triskelion

D507J09
Hurricane

D507J10

D507J11

D507J12

D507J13

D507J14

D507J15

D507J16

D507J17

D507J18

D507J19

D507J20

D507J21

D507J22

D507J23

D507J24

D507J25

D507J26

D507J27

D507J28

D507J29

D507J30

Designs
- Optical

D507**K**01

D507**K**02

D507**K**03

D507**K**04

D507**K**05
Sphere

D507**K**06

D507**K**07

D507**K**08

D507**K**09

D507**K**10

D507**K**11

D507**K**12

D507**K**13

D507**K**14

D507**K**15

D507**K**16

D507**K**17

D507**K**18

D507**K**19

D507**K**20

D507**K**21

D507**K**22

D507**K**23

D507**K**24

D507**K**25

- General

D507**K**26
No Entry

D507**K**27
Tri-radial

D507**K**28
Triquetrum

D507**K**29
Peace

D507**K**30

Designs
- General
continued

D507L01

D507L02
Crosshairs

D507L03
Crosshairs

D507L04
Crosshairs

D507L05
Registration Mark

D507L06
Registration Mark

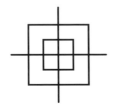

D507L07
Registration Mark

D507L08
Dart Board

D507L09
Dart Board
Dart

D507L10

D507L11
CD-Rom

D507L12
CD-Rom

D507L13
Ball Bearing
Engineering

D507L14
Fallout Shelter

D507L15
Radioactive
Danger

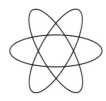

D507L16
Atomic
Nuclear

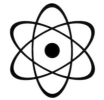

D507L17
Atomic
Nuclear

D507L18
Atomic
Electrons

D507L19

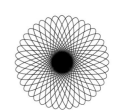

D507L20

Globes

D507L21
Atlantic Ocean
Geography

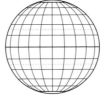

D507L22

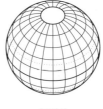

D507L23

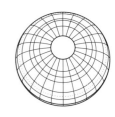

D507L24

D507L25

D507L26

D507L27

Globes
continued

D507**M**01

D507**M**02

D507**M**03

D507**M**04

D507**M**05
Sphere

Gears

D507**M**06

D507**M**07

D507**M**08

D507**M**09

D507**M**10

D507**M**11

D507**M**12

D507**M**13

D507**M**14

D507**M**15

D507**M**16

D507**M**17

D507**M**18

D507**M**19
Gears
Mechanics/Physics

D507**M**20

Radials

D507**M**21

D507**M**22

D507**M**23

D507**M**24

D507**M**25

D507**M**26

D507**M**27

D507**M**28

D507**M**29

D507**M**30

Radials
continued

D507N01

D507N02

D507N03

D507N04

D507N05

D507N06

D507N07

D507N08
Trefoil
The Holy Trinity

D507N09
Quatrefoil
Good Luck

D507N10

D507N11

D507N12

D507N13

D507N14

D507N15
Triquetra

D507N16

D507N17

D507N18

D507N19

D507N20

D507N21

D507N22

D507N23

D507N24

D507N25

D507N26
Sigil of the World
Gnosticism

D507N27

D507N28

D507N29

D507N30

Asterisks

D507**P**01   D507**P**02   D507**P**03   D507**P**04   D507**P**05

D507**P**06   D507**P**07   D507**P**08   D507**P**09   D507**P**10

D507**P**11   D507**P**12   D507**P**13   D507**P**14   D507**P**15

D507**P**16   D507**P**17   D507**P**18   D507**P**19   D507**P**20

D507**P**21   D507**P**22   D507**P**23   D507**P**24   D507**P**25

D507**P**26   D507**P**27   D507**P**28   D507**P**29   D507**P**30

Asterisks
continued

D507**Q**02

D507**Q**03

D507**Q**04

D507**Q**05

D507**Q**06

D507**Q**07

D507**Q**01

D507**Q**08

D507**Q**09

D507**Q**10

D507**Q**11

D507**Q**12

D507**Q**13

D507**Q**14

Note: All images
are available as
fully editable vector
image files: see
page 286 or www.
ultimatesymbol.com

D507**Q**15

D507**Q**16

D507**Q**17

D507**Q**18

D507**Q**19

Compass Faces

D507**R**01
Navigation

D507**R**02

D507**R**03

D507**R**04

D507**R**05

D507**R**06

D507**R**07

D507**R**08

D507**R**09

D507**R**10

D507**R**11

D507**R**12

D507**R**13

D507**R**14

D507**R**15

D507**R**16

D507**R**17

D507**R**18

D507**R**19

D507**R**20

D507**R**21

D507**R**22
North Star

D507**R**23

D507**R**24
Mapping
Due North

D507**R**25
Mapping
Due North

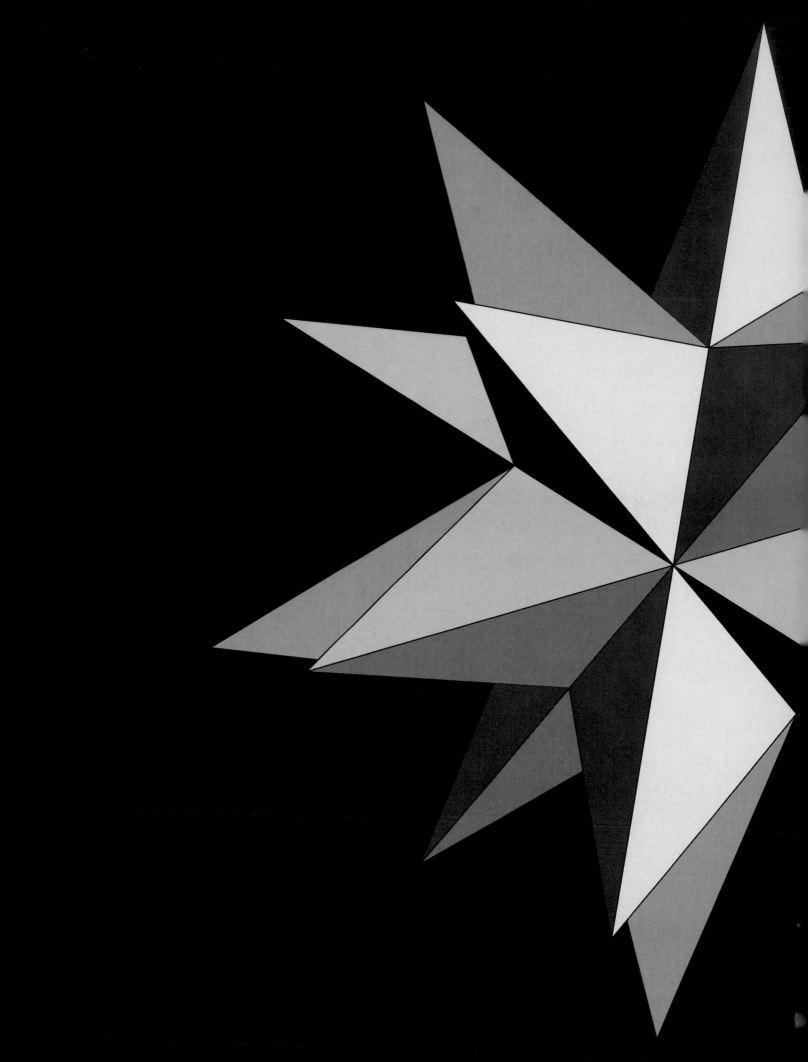

8

Crosses

D508**A**01

D508**A**02

D508**A**03
Greek
St. George

D508**A**04

D508**A**05

D508**A**06

D508**A**07

D508**A**08
Voided

D508**A**09

D508**A**10

D508**A**11
Wavy Voided

D508**A**12

D508**A**13

D508**A**14
Interlaced

D508**A**15

D508**A**16

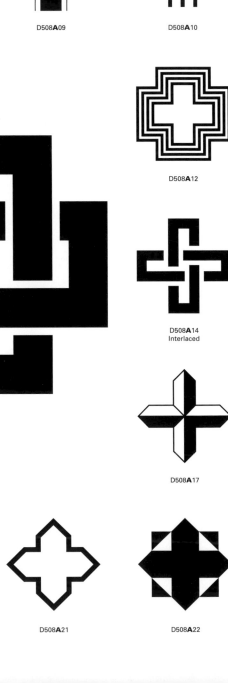

D508**A**17

D508**A**18

D508**A**19

D508**A**20

D508**A**21

D508**A**22

*

✳ Composed of Separate Shapes

Crosses
continued

D508B01

D508B02
St. Andrew
St. Patrick

D508B03

D508B04

D508B05

D508B06

D508B07

D508B08
Infinite
Eternity

D508B09
Maltese
Variant

D508B10

D508B11
Formée

D508B12
Formée

D508B13

D508B14

D508B15
Formée

D508B16
Maltese
Variant

D508B17

D508B18

D508B19
Pattée Convex
Voided

D508B20

D508B21

D508B22

D508B23
Maltese

D508B24

D508B25
Patonce Pattée

D508B26
Patonce Pattée

D508B27
Patonce Pattée

D508B28
Patonce Pattée

D508B29
Fleurée
(Fleury)

D508B30
Bottonée

Crosses
continued

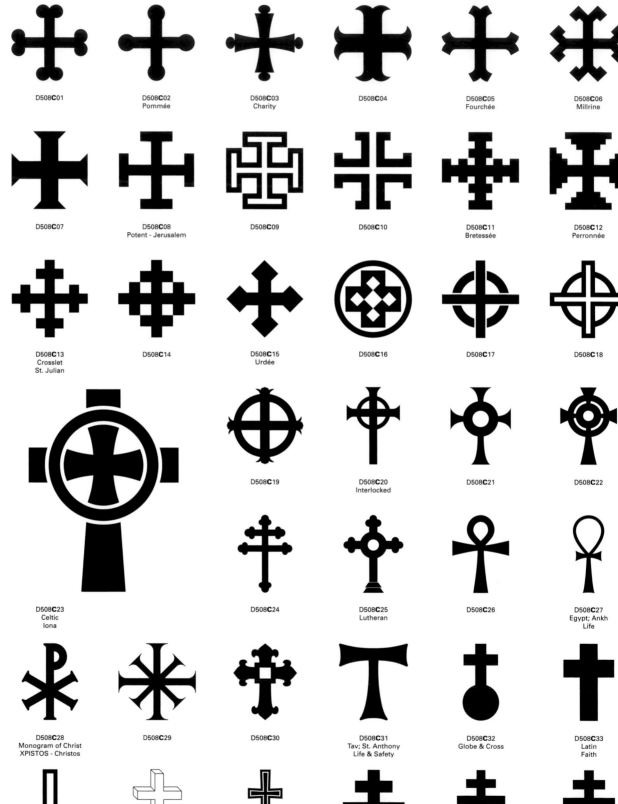

D508**C**01

D508**C**02
Pommée

D508**C**03
Charity

D508**C**04

D508**C**05
Fourchée

D508**C**06
Millrine

D508**C**07

D508**C**08
Potent - Jerusalem

D508**C**09

D508**C**10

D508**C**11
Bretessée

D508**C**12
Perronnée

D508**C**13
Crosslet
St. Julian

D508**C**14

D508**C**15
Urdée

D508**C**16

D508**C**17

D508**C**18

D508**C**23
Celtic
Iona

D508**C**19

D508**C**20
Interlocked

D508**C**21

D508**C**22

D508**C**24

D508**C**25
Lutheran

D508**C**26

D508**C**27
Egypt; Ankh
Life

D508**C**28
Monogram of Christ
XPISTOS - Christos

D508**C**29

D508**C**30

D508**C**31
Tav; St. Anthony
Life & Safety

D508**C**32
Globe & Cross

D508**C**33
Latin
Faith

Note: All images
are available as
fully editable vector
image files: see
page 286 or www.
ultimatesymbol.com

D508**C**34
St. Peter

D508**C**35

D508**C**36

D508**C**37
Greek Orthodox
Patriarchal

D508**C**38
Russian Orthodox
Triple-Beam Cross

D508**C**39
Papal

Hearts

D508**D**01
Charity

D508**D**02

D508**D**03

D508**D**04

D508**D**05

D508**D**06

D508**D**07

D508**D**08

D508**D**09

D508**D**10

D508**D**11

D508**D**12

D508**D**13

D508**D**14

D508**D**15

D508**D**16

D508**D**17

D508**D**18

D508**D**19

D508**D**20

D508**D**21

D508**D**22

D508**D**23

D508**D**24
Interlocked

Droplets
Teardrops

D508**D**25
Heart

D508**D**26
Club

D508**D**27
Spade

D508**D**28
Diamond

D508**D**29

D508**D**30

D508**D**31

D508**D**32

D508**D**33

D508**D**34

D508**D**35

D508**D**36

Eggs

D508E01   D508E02   D508E03   D508E04   D508E05   D508E06

Pear Shapes

D508E07   D508E08   D508E09   D508E10   D508E11   D508E12
                                                                        Guitar

D508E13   D508E14   D508E15   D508E16   D508E17   D508E18
            Guitar   Violin   Dulcimer   Gourd
                                                Taoist Necromancy

General

D508E19   D508E20   D508E21   D508E22   D508E23   D508E24
            Apple

D508E25   D508E26   D508E27   D508E28   D508E29   D508E30

D508E31   D508E32   D508E33   D508E34   D508E35   D508E36
Hourglass   Hourglass   Hourglass   Keyhole
                        Time

D508E37   D508E38   D508E39   D508E40   D508E41   D508E42

Geometrics
- Arches

- Parabolas

- Ovals

- Ellipses

- Elliptical Shapes

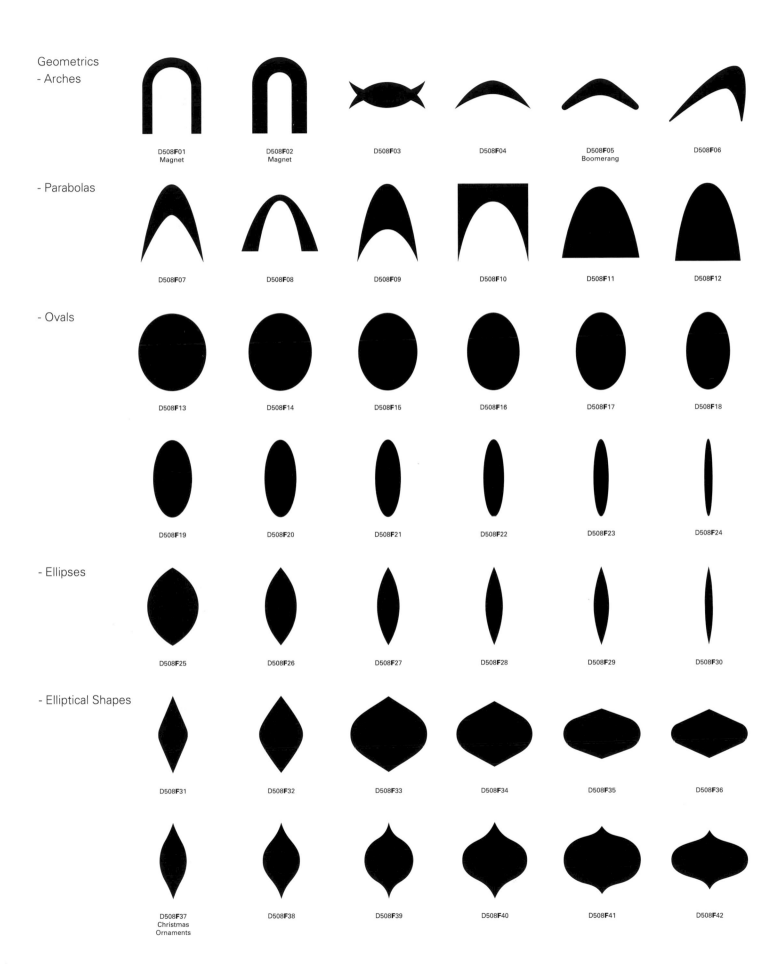

D508F01
Magnet

D508F02
Magnet

D508F03

D508F04

D508F05
Boomerang

D508F06

D508F07

D508F08

D508F09

D508F10

D508F11

D508F12

D508F13

D508F14

D508F15

D508F16

D508F17

D508F18

D508F19

D508F20

D508F21

D508F22

D508F23

D508F24

D508F25

D508F26

D508F27

D508F28

D508F29

D508F30

D508F31

D508F32

D508F33

D508F34

D508F35

D508F36

D508F37
Christmas
Ornaments

D508F38

D508F39

D508F40

D508F41

D508F42

Geometrics
- Circles

D508**G**01
Cylinder

D508**G**02
Cylinder

D508**G**03

D508**G**04
Three-Quarter Circle

D508**G**05
Half Circle

D508**G**06
Quarter Circle

D508**G**07 *

D508**G**08 *

D508**G**09 *

D508**G**10 *

D508**G**11 *

D508**G**12 *

- Triangles

D508**G**13
Conical

D508**G**14
Isosceles

D508**G**15
Isosceles

D508**G**16
Equilateral
Internal Angle: 60°

D508**G**17

D508**G**18

D508**G**19 *

D508**G**20

D508**G**21

D508**G**22
Scalene, Obtuse

D508**G**23

D508**G**24

D508**G**25

D508**G**26

D508**G**27

D508**G**28

D508**G**29

D508**G**30

D508**G**31

D508**G**32

D508**G**33

D508**G**34

D508**G**35

D508**G**36

D508**G**37

D508**G**38

D508**G**39

D508**G**40

D508**G**41 *
Water-Fire Principle

D508**G**42

* Composed of Separate Shapes

Geometrics
- Triangles
continued

D508H01

D508H02

D508H03

D508H04

D508H05 *

D508H06

D508H07 *

D508H08 *

D508H09 *
Pyramid
Tetrahedron

D508H10
Pyramid

D508H11 *
Pyramid

D508H12
Pyramid

- Pentagons
- Crystals
- Diamonds

D508H13
Prism

D508H14
Prism

D508H15 *

D508H16
Internal Angle: 108°

D508H17

D508H18 *

D508H19

D508H20 *

D508H21

D508H22

D508H23

D508H24

D508H25

D508H26

D508H27

D508H28

D508H29

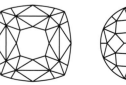

D508H30 *

Diamond Cuts

D508H31

D508H32
Emerald

D508H33
Marquise

D508H34
Oval

D508H35
Pear

D508H36
Heart

D508H37
Round Brilliant

D508H38
Long Hexagon

D508H39
Pentagon

D508H40
Trilliant

D508H41
Lisbon

D508H42
Jubilee

* Composed of Separate Shapes

Geometrics
continued
- Quadrilaterals
- Squares
- Hexagons
- Polygons

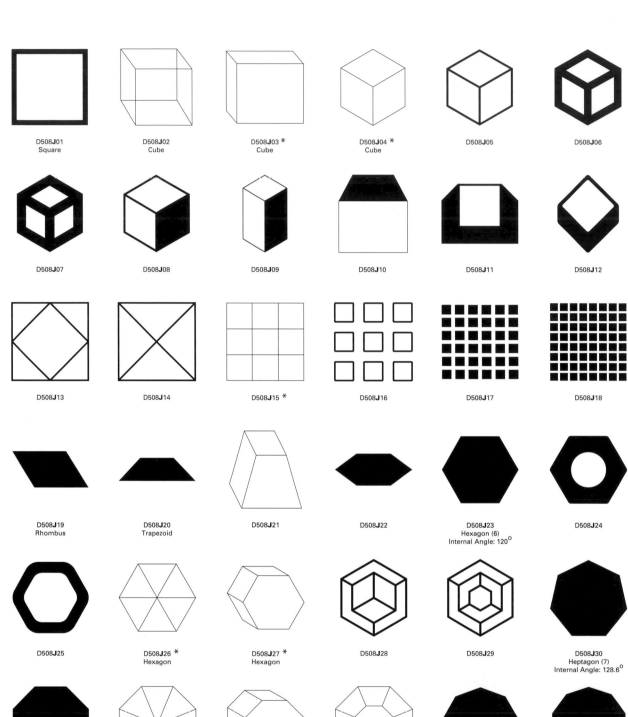

D508J01
Square

D508J02
Cube

D508J03 *
Cube

D508J04 *
Cube

D508J05

D508J06

D508J07

D508J08

D508J09

D508J10

D508J11

D508J12

D508J13

D508J14

D508J15 *

D508J16

D508J17

D508J18

D508J19
Rhombus

D508J20
Trapezoid

D508J21

D508J22

D508J23
Hexagon (6)
Internal Angle: 120°

D508J24

D508J25

D508J26 *
Hexagon

D508J27 *
Hexagon

D508J28

D508J29

D508J30
Heptagon (7)
Internal Angle: 128.6°

D508J31
Octagon (8)
Internal Angle: 135°

D508J32 *
Octagon

D508J33 *
Octagon

D508J34 *
Octagon

D508J35
Nonagon (9)
Internal Angle: 140°

D508J36
Decagon (10)
Internal Angle: 144°

D508J37 *
Decagon

D508J38
Undecagon (11)
Internal Angle: 147.3°

D508J39
Dodecagon (12)
Internal Angle: 150°

D508J40 *
Dodecagon

D508J41
Pyramidal Coil

D508J42
Coil

* Composed of Separate Shapes

Geometrics
- Polyhedra

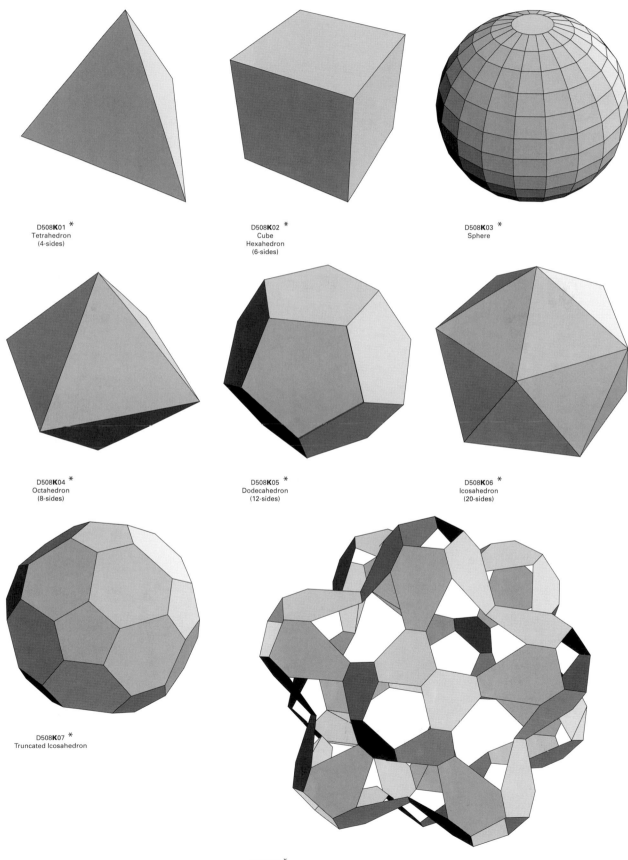

D508**K**01 *
Tetrahedron
(4-sides)

D508**K**02 *
Cube
Hexahedron
(6-sides)

D508**K**03 *
Sphere

D508**K**04 *
Octahedron
(8-sides)

D508**K**05 *
Dodecahedron
(12-sides)

D508**K**06 *
Icosahedron
(20-sides)

D508**K**07 *
Truncated Icosahedron

D508**K**08 *
Open Truncated Stellated
Dodecahedron

* Composed of Separate Shapes

Geometrics
- Polyhedra
continued

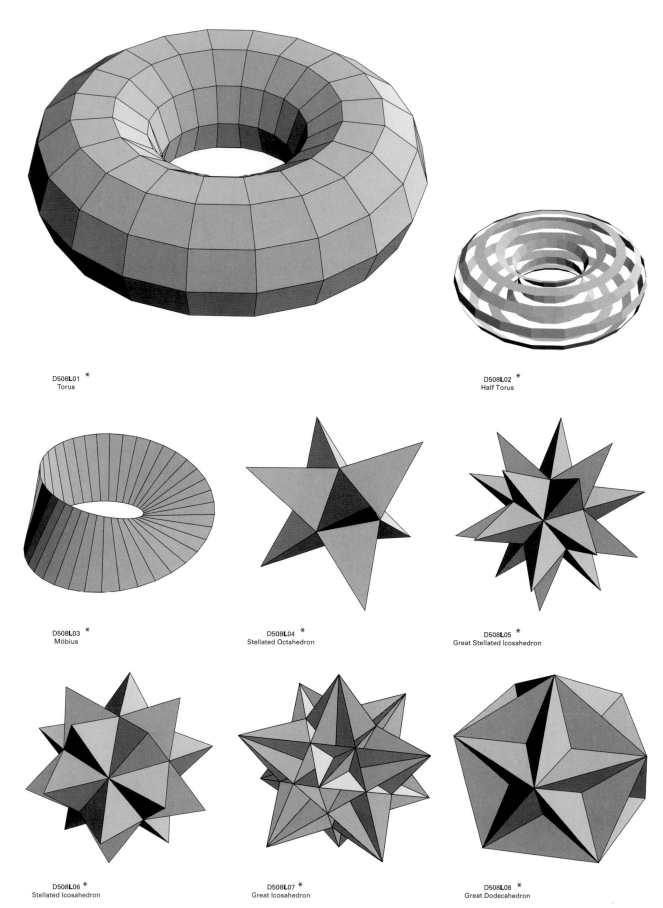

D508L01 *
Torus

D508L02 *
Half Torus

D508L03 *
Möbius

D508L04 *
Stellated Octahedron

D508L05 *
Great Stellated Icosahedron

D508L06 *
Stellated Icosahedron

D508L07 *
Great Icosahedron

D508L08 *
Great Dodecahedron

* Composed of Separate Shapes

Geometrics
continued
- Isometrics

D508M01

D508M02

D508M03

D508M04

D508M05

D508M06

D508M07

D508M08

D508M09

D508M10

D508M11

D508M12

D508M13

D508M14

D508M15

D508M16

D508M17

D508M18

D508M19

D508M20

D508M21

D508M22

Squares
- Optical

D508N01

D508N02

D508N03

D508N04

D508N05

D508N06

D508N07

D508N08

D508N09

D508N10

D508N11

D508N12

D508N13

D508N14

D508N15

D508N16

D508N17

D508N18

D508N19

D508N20

D508N21

D508N22

D508N23

D508N24

D508N25

D508N26

D508N27

General

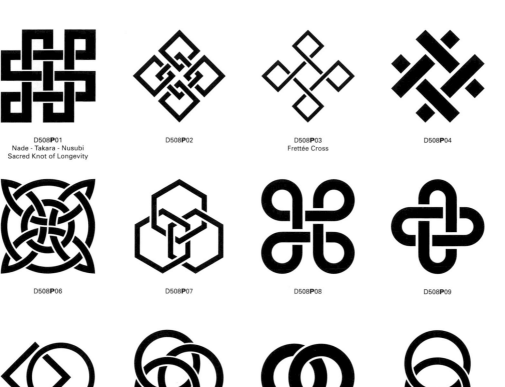

D508P01
Nade - Takara - Nusubi
Sacred Knot of Longevity

D508P02

D508P03
Frettée Cross

D508P04

D508P05

D508P06

D508P07

D508P08

D508P09

D508P10

D508P11

D508P12

D508P13

D508P14

D508P15

D508P16

D508P17

D508P18

D508P19

D508P20

Puzzle Pieces

D508P21

D508P22

D508P23

D508P24

D508P25

D508P26

D508P27

D508P28

D508P29

Shields
Badges

D508Q01

D508Q02   D508Q03   D508Q04   D508Q05

D508Q06   D508Q07   D508Q08   D508Q09

D508Q10   D508Q11   D508Q12   D508Q13   D508Q14   D508Q15

D508Q16   D508Q17   D508Q18   D508Q19   D508Q20   D508Q21

D508Q22   D508Q23   D508Q24   D508Q25   D508Q26   D508Q27

D508Q28   D508Q29   D508Q30   D508Q31   D508Q32   D508Q33

Note: All images
are available as
fully editable vector
image files: see
page 286 or www.
ultimatesymbol.com

D508Q34   D508Q35   D508Q36   D508Q37   D508Q38   D508Q39

Shields
Badges
continued

Tombstones
Headstones

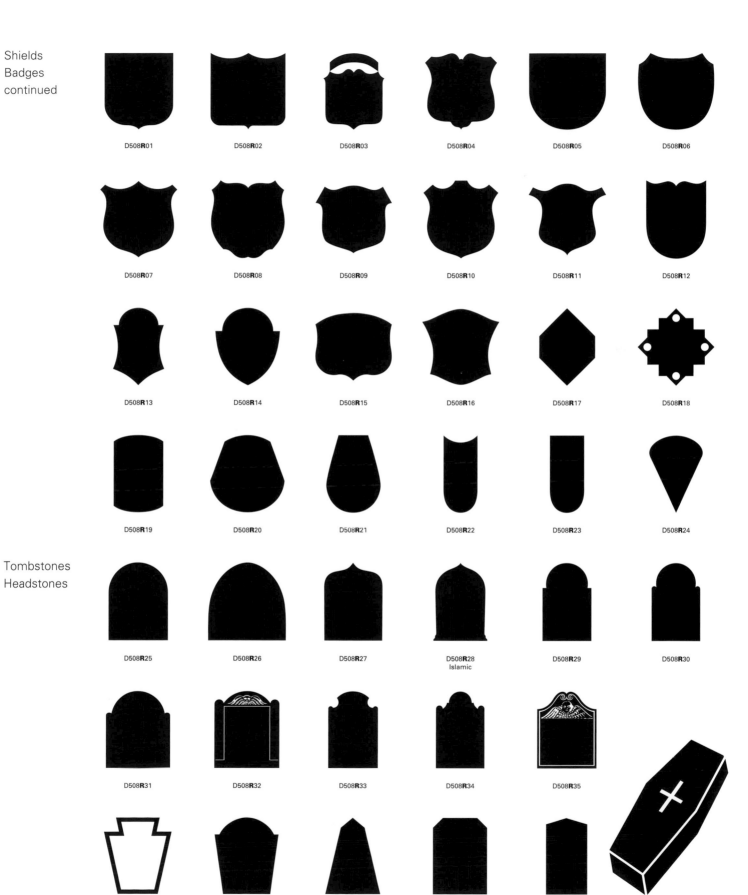

D508R01   D508R02   D508R03   D508R04   D508R05   D508R06

D508R07   D508R08   D508R09   D508R10   D508R11   D508R12

D508R13   D508R14   D508R15   D508R16   D508R17   D508R18

D508R19   D508R20   D508R21   D508R22   D508R23   D508R24

D508R25   D508R26   D508R27   D508R28
Islamic   D508R29   D508R30

D508R31   D508R32   D508R33   D508R34   D508R35

D508R36
Keystone   D508R37   D508R38   D508R39   D508R40   D508R41
Coffin, Casket
Death

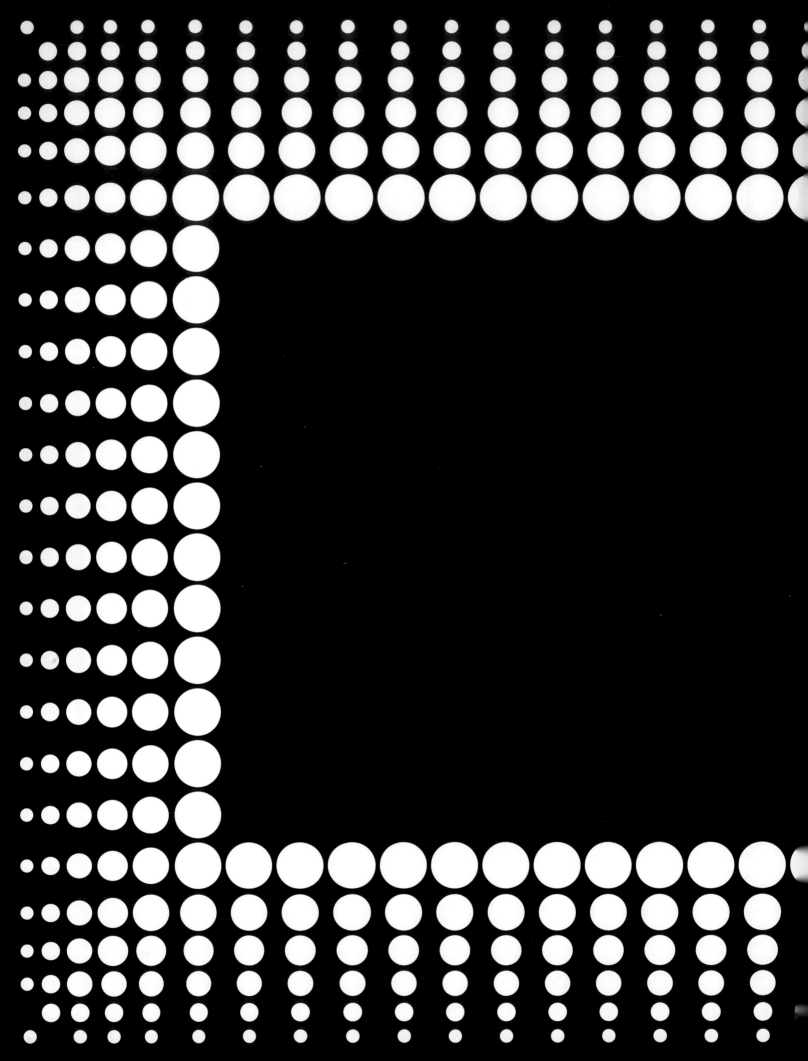

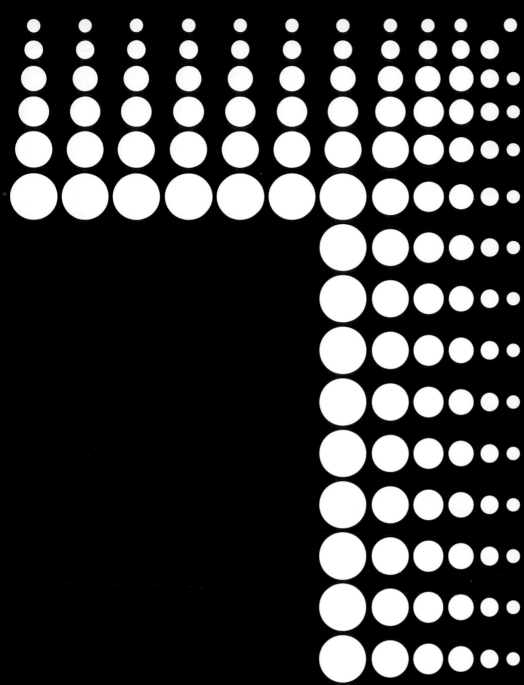

9

Frames
- Varied Weight
  Rules

D509**A**01

D509**A**02

D509**A**03

D509**A**04

D509**A**05

D509**A**06

D509**A**07

D509**A**08

D509**A**09

D509**A**10

D509**A**11

D509**A**12

D509**A**13

D509**A**14

D509**A**15

D509**A**16

D509**A**17

Frames
- Varied Weight
  Rules
  continued

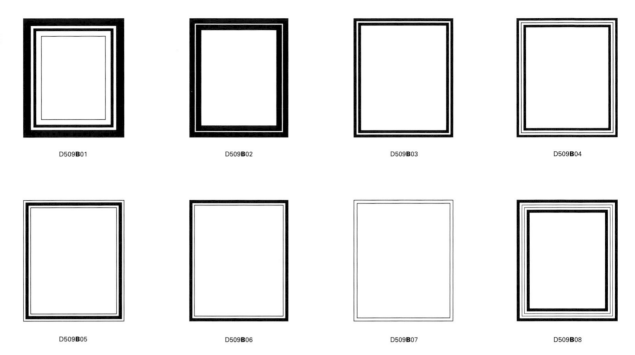

D509**B**01   D509**B**02   D509**B**03   D509**B**04

D509**B**05   D509**B**06   D509**B**07   D509**B**08

- General
- Art Deco

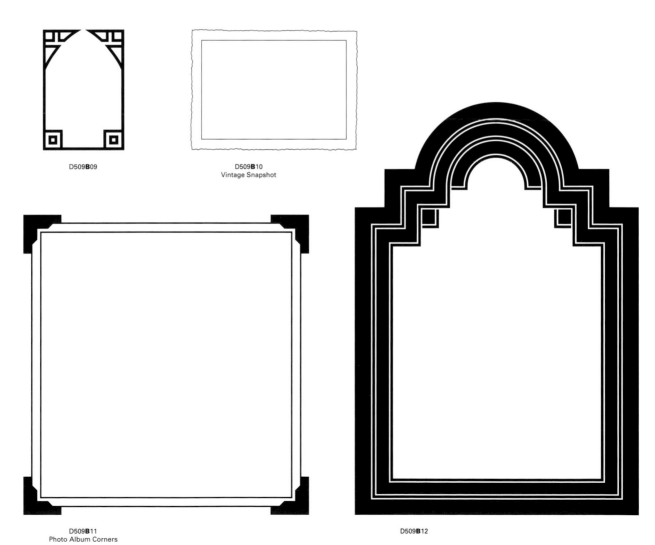

D509**B**09

D509**B**10
Vintage Snapshot

D509**B**11
Photo Album Corners

D509**B**12

Frames
- Art Deco
  continued

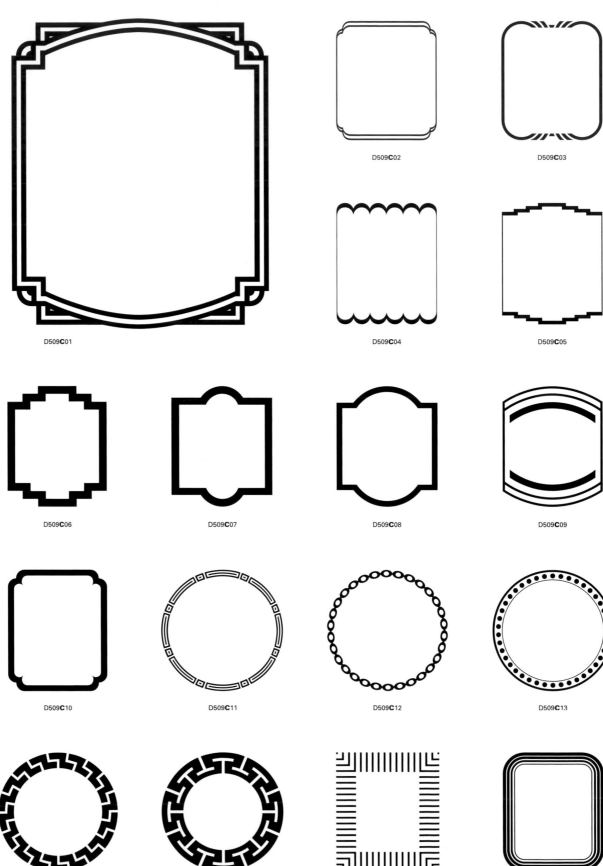

D509**C**01

D509**C**02

D509**C**03

D509**C**04

D509**C**05

D509**C**06

D509**C**07

D509**C**08

D509**C**09

D509**C**10

D509**C**11

D509**C**12

D509**C**13

Note: All images
are available as
fully editable vector
image files: see
page 286 or www.
ultimatesymbol.com

D509**C**14

D509**C**15

D509**C**16

D509**C**17

Frames
- Ornate

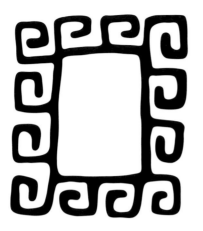

D509**D**01

D509**D**02

D509**D**03

D509**D**04

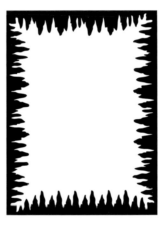

D509**D**05

D509**D**06

D509**D**07

D509**D**08

Frames
- Ornate
  continued

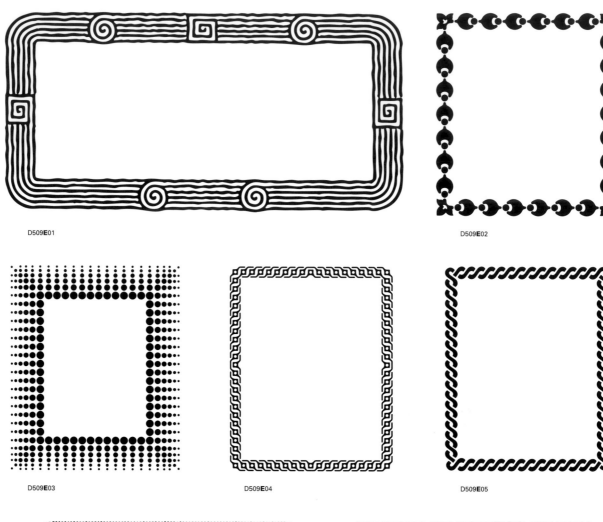

D509E01

D509E02

D509E03

D509E04

D509E05

D509E06

D509E07

Frames
- Ornate
  continued
- Circles

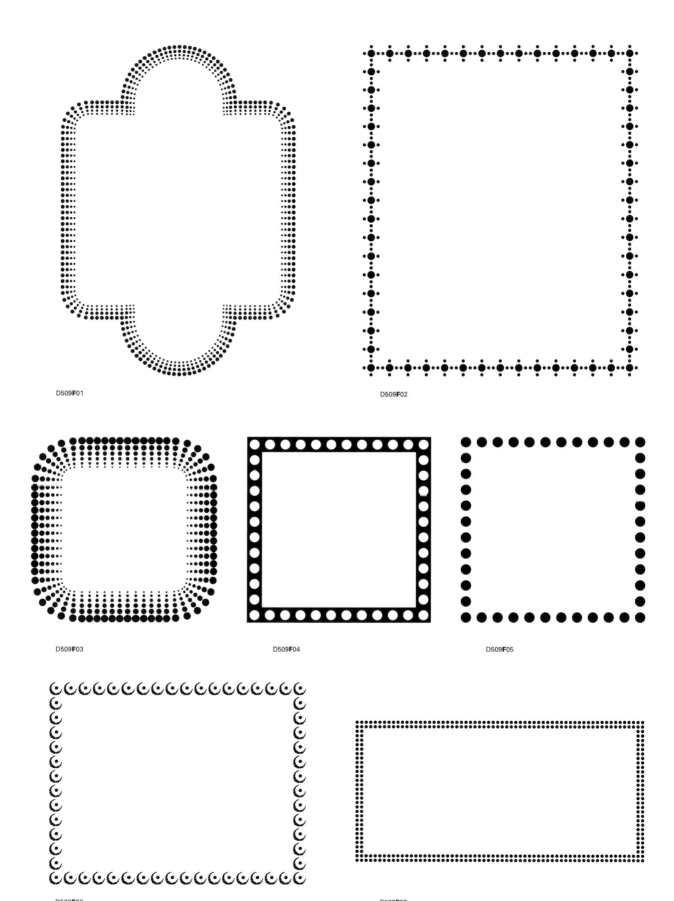

D509F01

D509F02

D509F03

D509F04

D509F05

D509F06

D509F07

Frames
- Ornate
- Circles
  continued

D509**G**01

D509**G**02

D509**G**03

D509**G**04

D509**G**05

D509**G**06

D509**G**07
Thorns

D509**G**08

Frames
- Ornate
  continued
- Floral

D509**H**01

D509**H**02

D509**H**03

D509**H**04

D509**H**05

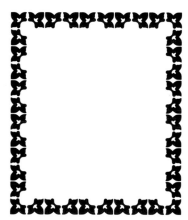

D509**H**06

D509**H**07

D509**H**08

Frames
- Ornate
- Floral
  continued

D509J01

D509J02

D509J03

D509J04

D509J05

D509J06

D509J07

Frames
- Ornate
  continued

D509**K**01

D509**K**02

D509**K**03
Curtains

D509**K**04
Curtains

D509**K**05
Proscenium

D509**K**06
Ribbon

D509**K**07
Ribbon

D509**K**08

D509**K**09

D509**K**10

D509**K**11

D509**K**12

D509**K**13

Frames
- Ornate
  continued
- Art Nouveau

D509L01   D509L02   D509L03   D509L04

D509L05   D509L06   D509L07   D509L08

D509L09   D509L10   D509L11   D509L12

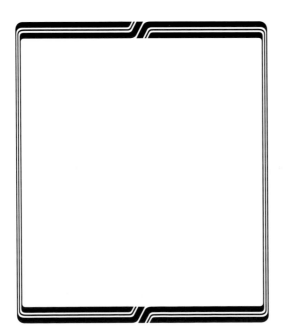

D509L13   D509L14

Frames
Corners
- Ornate
- Art Nouveau
   continued

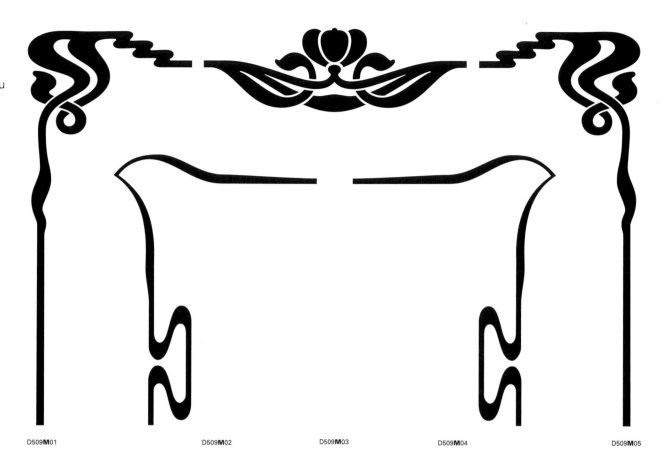

D509M01   D509M02   D509M03   D509M04   D509M05

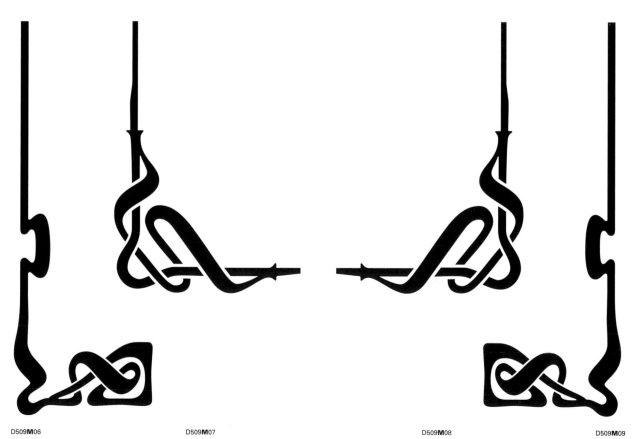

D509M06   D509M07   D509M08   D509M09

Frames
Corners
- Ornate
- Art Nouveau
  continued

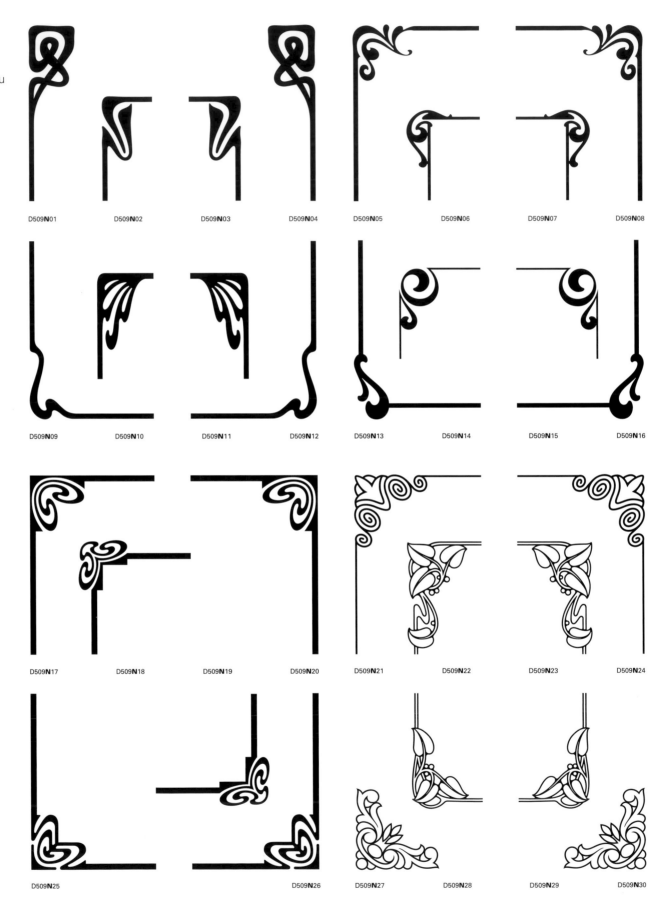

D509N01   D509N02   D509N03   D509N04   D509N05   D509N06   D509N07   D509N08

D509N09   D509N10   D509N11   D509N12   D509N13   D509N14   D509N15   D509N16

D509N17   D509N18   D509N19   D509N20   D509N21   D509N22   D509N23   D509N24

D509N25   D509N26   D509N27   D509N28   D509N29   D509N30

Frames
Corners
- Ornate
- Art Nouveau
continued

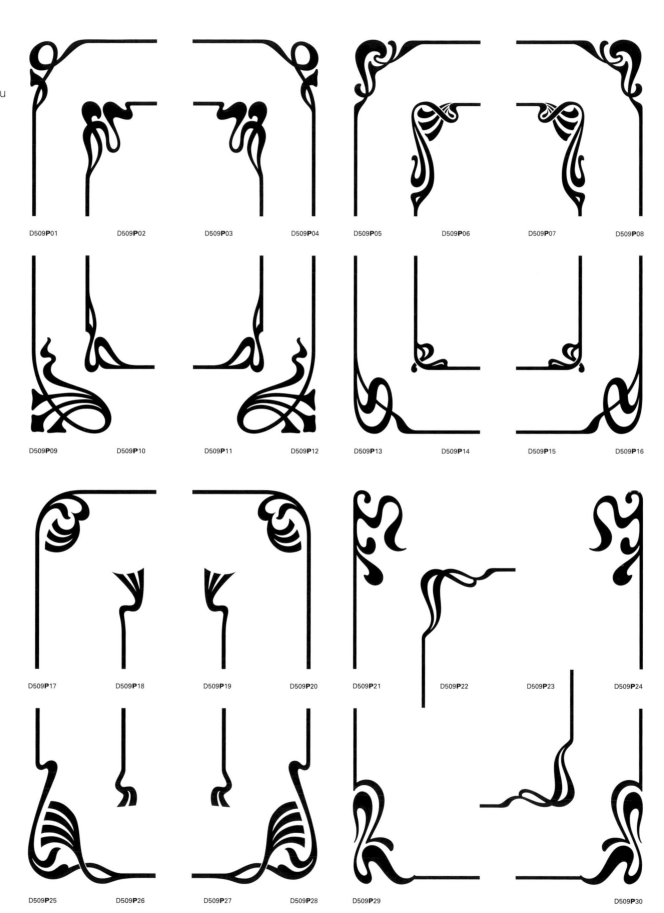

D509**P**01 D509**P**02 D509**P**03 D509**P**04 D509**P**05 D509**P**06 D509**P**07 D509**P**08

D509**P**09 D509**P**10 D509**P**11 D509**P**12 D509**P**13 D509**P**14 D509**P**15 D509**P**16

D509**P**17 D509**P**18 D509**P**19 D509**P**20 D509**P**21 D509**P**22 D509**P**23 D509**P**24

D509**P**25 D509**P**26 D509**P**27 D509**P**28 D509**P**29 D509**P**30

Frames
Corners
- Ornate
- Art Nouveau
  continued

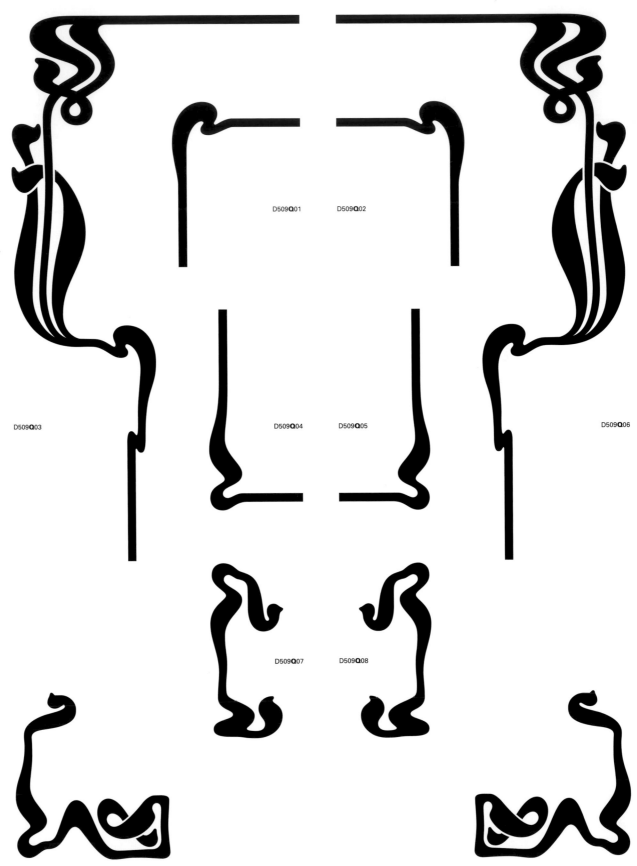

D509Q01   D509Q02

D509Q03   D509Q04   D509Q05   D509Q06

D509Q07   D509Q08

D509Q09   D509Q10

Frames
Corners
- Ornate
- Art Nouveau
  continued

D509R01   D509R02   D509R03   D509R04   D509R05   D509R06   D509R07   D509R08

D509R09   D509R10   D509R11   D509R12   D509R13   D509R14   D509R15   D509R16

D509R17   D509R18   D509R19   D509R20   D509R21   D509R22   D509R23   D509R24

D509R25   D509R26   D509R27   D509R28   D509R29   D509R30   D509R31   D509R32

Frames
Corners
- Ornate
- Art Nouveau
  continued

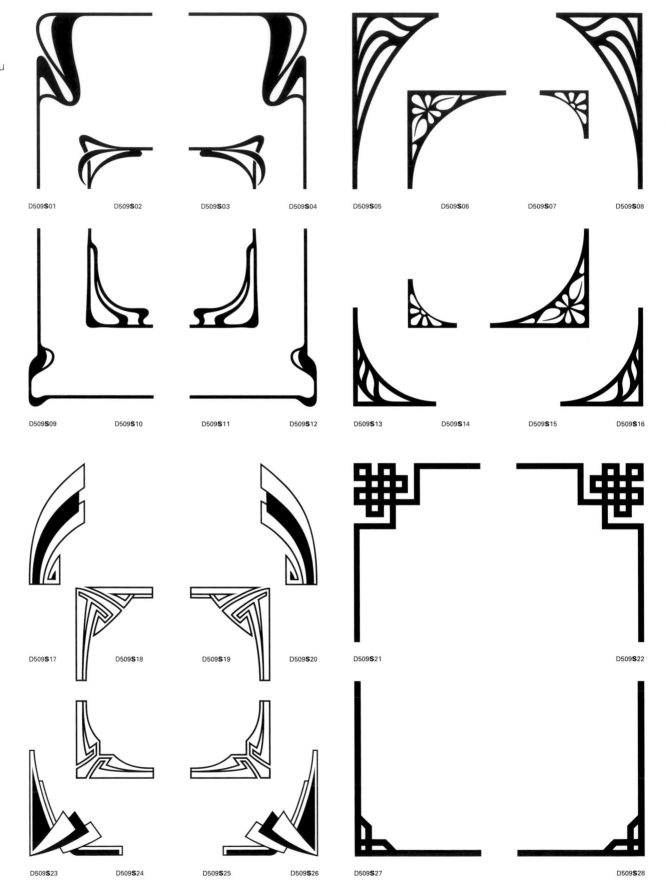

D509**S**01   D509**S**02   D509**S**03   D509**S**04   D509**S**05   D509**S**06   D509**S**07   D509**S**08

D509**S**09   D509**S**10   D509**S**11   D509**S**12   D509**S**13   D509**S**14   D509**S**15   D509**S**16

D509**S**17   D509**S**18   D509**S**19   D509**S**20   D509**S**21   D509**S**22

D509**S**23   D509**S**24   D509**S**25   D509**S**26   D509**S**27   D509**S**28

Corners
- Geometric

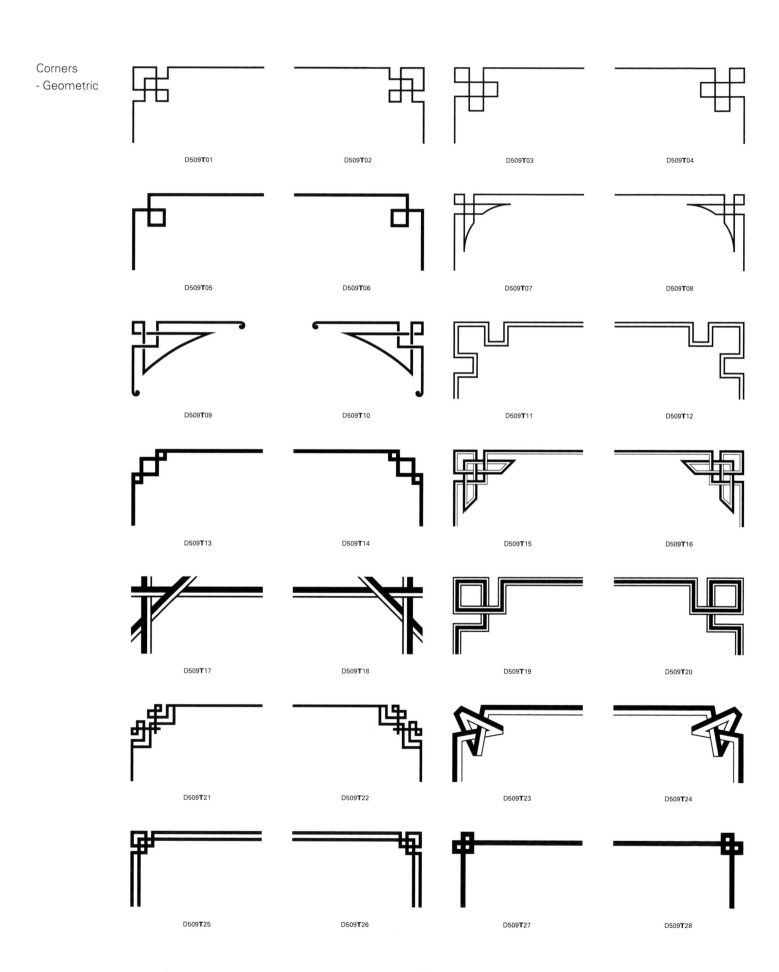

D509**T**01   D509**T**02   D509**T**03   D509**T**04

D509**T**05   D509**T**06   D509**T**07   D509**T**08

D509**T**09   D509**T**10   D509**T**11   D509**T**12

D509**T**13   D509**T**14   D509**T**15   D509**T**16

D509**T**17   D509**T**18   D509**T**19   D509**T**20

D509**T**21   D509**T**22   D509**T**23   D509**T**24

D509**T**25   D509**T**26   D509**T**27   D509**T**28

Corners
- Geometric
continued

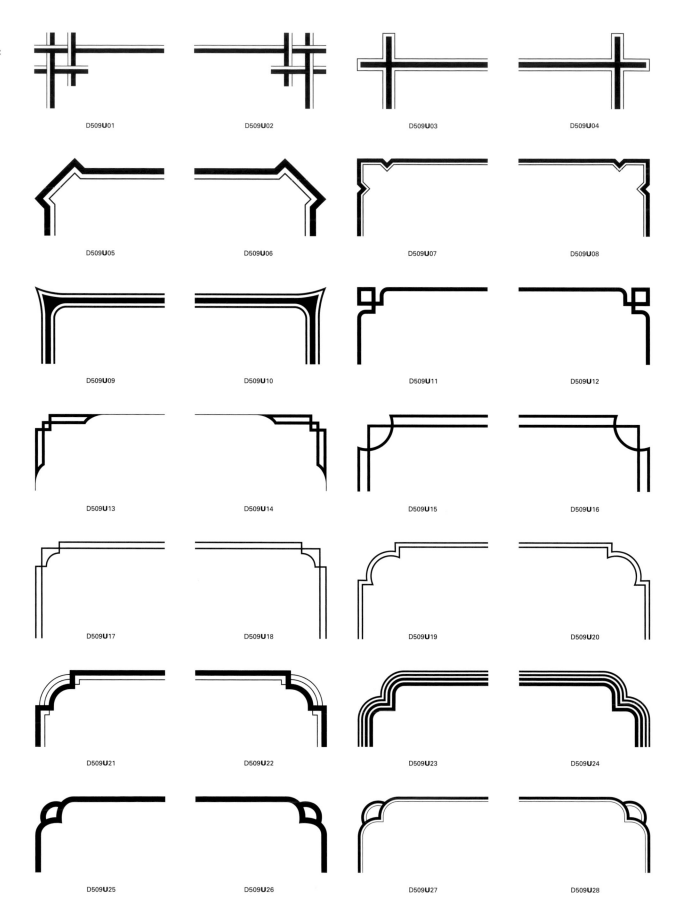

D509**U**01   D509**U**02   D509**U**03   D509**U**04

D509**U**05   D509**U**06   D509**U**07   D509**U**08

D509**U**09   D509**U**10   D509**U**11   D509**U**12

D509**U**13   D509**U**14   D509**U**15   D509**U**16

D509**U**17   D509**U**18   D509**U**19   D509**U**20

D509**U**21   D509**U**22   D509**U**23   D509**U**24

D509**U**25   D509**U**26   D509**U**27   D509**U**28

Corners
- Geometric
  continued
- Art Deco

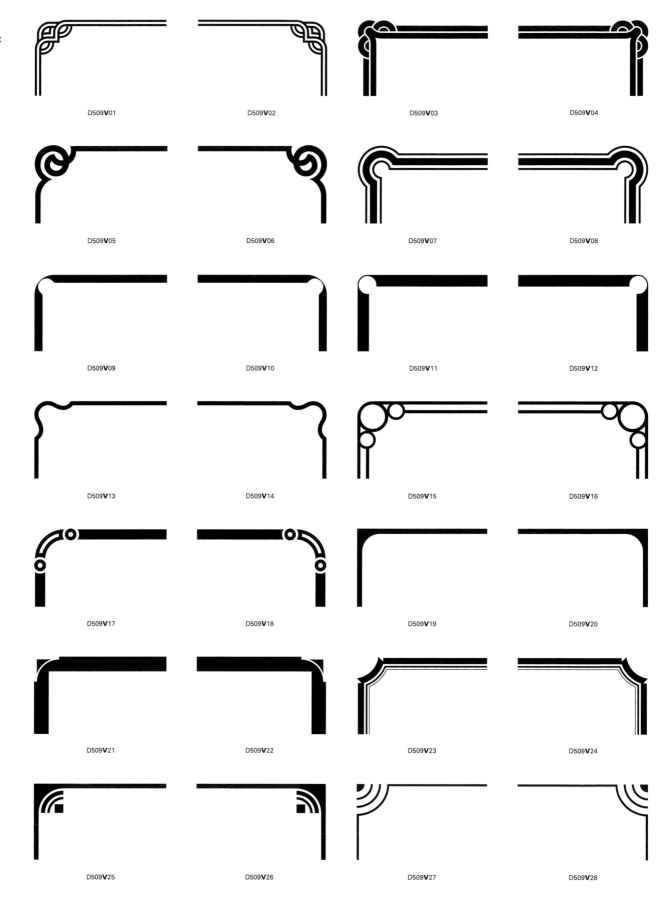

D509**V**01   D509**V**02   D509**V**03   D509**V**04

D509**V**05   D509**V**06   D509**V**07   D509**V**08

D509**V**09   D509**V**10   D509**V**11   D509**V**12

D509**V**13   D509**V**14   D509**V**15   D509**V**16

D509**V**17   D509**V**18   D509**V**19   D509**V**20

D509**V**21   D509**V**22   D509**V**23   D509**V**24

D509**V**25   D509**V**26   D509**V**27   D509**V**28

Corners
- Geometric
- Art Deco
continued

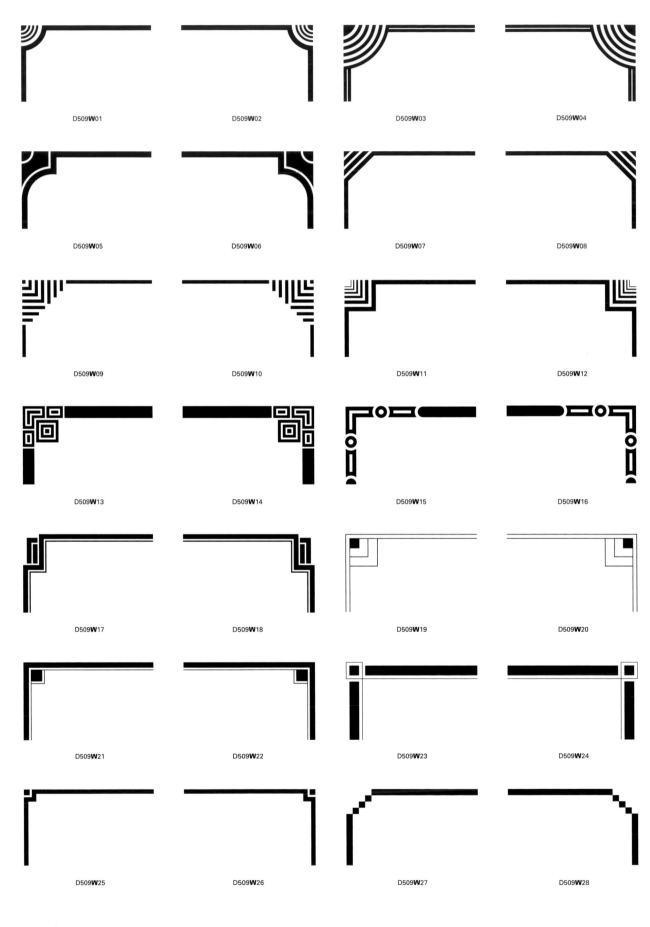

D509**W**01

D509**W**02

D509**W**03

D509**W**04

D509**W**05

D509**W**06

D509**W**07

D509**W**08

D509**W**09

D509**W**10

D509**W**11

D509**W**12

D509**W**13

D509**W**14

D509**W**15

D509**W**16

D509**W**17

D509**W**18

D509**W**19

D509**W**20

D509**W**21

D509**W**22

D509**W**23

D509**W**24

D509**W**25

D509**W**26

D509**W**27

D509**W**28

Corners
- Geometric
- Art Deco
  continued

D509**X**01

D509**X**02

D509**X**03

D509**X**04

D509**X**05

D509**X**06

D509**X**07

D509**X**08

D509**X**09

D509**X**10

D509**X**11

D509**X**12

D509**X**13

D509**X**14

D509**X**15

D509**X**16

D509**X**17

D509**X**18

D509**X**19

D509**X**20

D509**X**21

D509**X**22

D509**X**23

D509**X**24

D509**X**25

D509**X**26

D509**X**27

D509**X**28

Corners
continued
- Ornate

D509**Y**01   D509**Y**02   D509**Y**03   D509**Y**04

D509**Y**05   D509**Y**06   D509**Y**07   D509**Y**08

D509**Y**09   D509**Y**10   D509**Y**11   D509**Y**12

D509**Y**13   D509**Y**14   D509**Y**15   D509**Y**16

D509**Y**17   D509**Y**18   D509**Y**19   D509**Y**20

D509**Y**21   D509**Y**22   D509**Y**23   D509**Y**24

D509**Y**25   D509**Y**26   D509**Y**27   D509**Y**28

Corners
- Ornate
continued

D509**Z**01   D509**Z**02   D509**Z**03   D509**Z**04

D509**Z**05   D509**Z**06   D509**Z**07   D509**Z**08

D509**Z**09   D509**Z**10   D509**Z**11   D509**Z**12

D509**Z**13   D509**Z**14   D509**Z**15   D509**Z**16

D509**Z**17   D509**Z**18   D509**Z**19   D509**Z**20

D509**Z**21   D509**Z**22   D509**Z**23   D509**Z**24

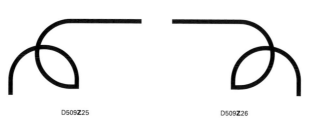

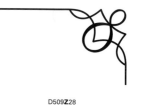

D509**Z**25   D509**Z**26   D509**Z**27   D509**Z**28

Corners
- Ornate
continued

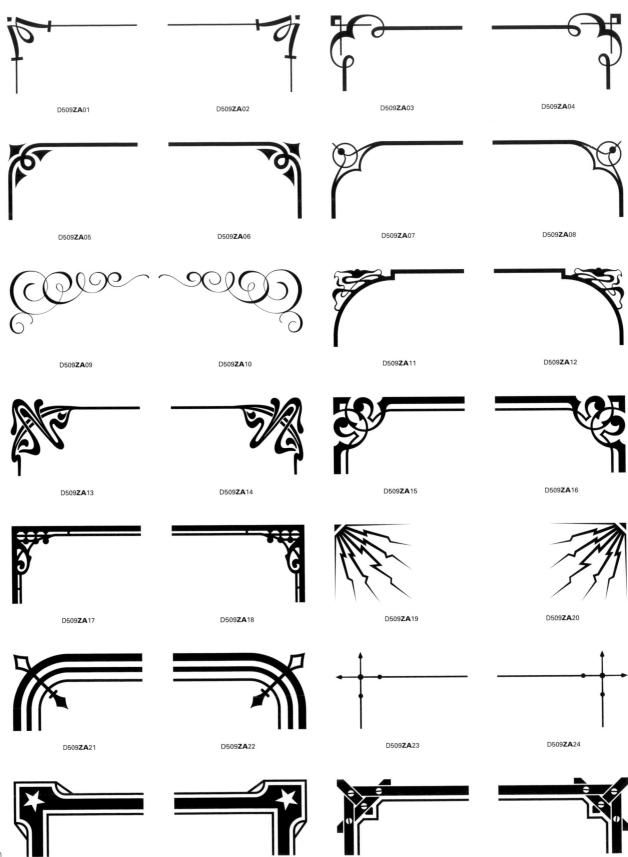

D509**ZA**01   D509**ZA**02   D509**ZA**03   D509**ZA**04

D509**ZA**05   D509**ZA**06   D509**ZA**07   D509**ZA**08

D509**ZA**09   D509**ZA**10   D509**ZA**11   D509**ZA**12

D509**ZA**13   D509**ZA**14   D509**ZA**15   D509**ZA**16

D509**ZA**17   D509**ZA**18   D509**ZA**19   D509**ZA**20

D509**ZA**21   D509**ZA**22   D509**ZA**23   D509**ZA**24

Note: All images
are available as
fully editable vector
image files: see
page 286 or www.
ultimatesymbol.com

D509**ZA**25   D509**ZA**26   D509**ZA**27   D509**ZA**28

Cornices

D509**ZB**01

D509**ZB**02

D509**ZB**03

D509**ZB**04

D509**ZB**05

D509**ZB**06

D509**ZB**07

D509**ZB**08

D509**ZB**09

D509**ZB**10

D509**ZB**11

D509**ZB**12

D509**ZB**13

D509**ZB**14

D509**ZB**15

D509**ZB**16

10

General
- Cornucopia
- Grapes
- Fruit

D510**A**01

D510**A**02

D510**A**03

D510**A**04

D510**A**05

D510**A**06

D510**A**07

D510**A**08

D510**A**09

D510**A**10

D510**A**11

D510**A**12

D510**A**13

D510**A**14

D510**A**15

D510**A**16

D510**A**17

D510**A**18

General
continued

D510**B**01

D510**B**02

D510**B**05

D510**B**03

D510**B**04

D510**B**06
Corn

D510**B**07

D510**B**08
Strawberry

D510**B**09

D510**B**10

D510**B**11

D510**B**12
Daisies

D510**B**13
Daisies

D510**B**14
Daisy

D510**B**15
Daisy

D510**B**16
Daisies

D510**B**17
Daisies

General
continued

D510**C**01

D510**C**02

D510**C**03

D510**C**04

D510**C**05

D510**C**06

D510**C**07

D510**C**08

Note: All images
are available as
fully editable vector
image files: see
page 286 or www.
ultimatesymbol.com

D510**C**09

D510**C**10

Leaves

D510**D**01
3-Leaf Clover

D510**D**02
3-Leaf Clover

D510**D**03

D510**D**04

D510**D**05

D510**D**06

D510**D**07

D510**D**08

D510**D**09

D510**D**10

D510**D**11

D510**D**12

D510**D**13

D510**D**14

D510**D**15

D510**D**16

D510**D**17

D510**D**18

D510**D**19

D510**D**20

Leaves
continued

D510E01

D510E02

D510E03

D510E04

Flowers

D510E05

D510E06

D510E07

D510E08

D510E09

D510E10

D510E11

D510E12

D510E13

D510E14

D510E15

D510E16

D510E17

D510E18

D510E19

D510E20

Flowers
continued

D510F01

D510F02

D510F03

D510F04

D510F05

D510F06

D510F07

D510F08

D510F09

D510F10

D510F11

D510F12

D510F13

D510F14

D510F15

D510F16

D510F17

D510F18

D510F19

D510F20

General

D510**G**01

D510**G**02

D510**G**03

D510**G**04

D510**G**05

D510**G**06

D510**G**07

D510**G**08

D510**G**09

D510**G**10

D510**G**11

D510**G**12

D510**G**13

D510**G**14

D510**G**15

D510**G**16

D510**G**17

D510**G**18

D510**G**19

General
continued

D510H01

D510H02

D510H03

D510H04

D510H05

D510H06

D510H07

D510H08

D510H09

D510H10

D510H11

D510H12

D510H13

D510H14

D510H15

D510H16

General
continued
- Wheat
- Laurels

D510J01

D510J02

D510J03

D510J04

D510J05

D510J06
Palm Leaf
Victory

D510J07
Laurel
Victory

D510J08

D510J09

D510J10

D510J11

D510J12

D510J13

D510J14

D510J15

D510J16

General
continued

D510**K**01

D510**K**02

D510**K**03

D510**K**04

D510**K**05

D510**K**06

D510**K**07

D510**K**08

D510**K**09

D510**K**10
Pear

D510**K**11
Pear

- Thistle
- Roses

D510**K**12

D510**K**13

D510**K**14

D510**K**15

D510**K**16

D510**K**17

D510**K**18

D510**K**19

General
- Roses
  continued
- Flowers

D510L01

D510L02

D510L03

D510L04

D510L05

D510L06

D510L07

D510L08

D510L09

D510L10

D510L11

D510L12

D510L13

D510L14

D510L15

D510L16

D510L17

D510L18

General
- Flowers
  continued

D510**M**01

D510**M**02

D510**M**03

D510**M**04

D510**M**05

D510**M**06

D510**M**07

D510**M**08

D510**M**09

D510**M**10

D510**M**11

D510**M**12

D510**M**13

D510**M**14

D510**M**15

D510**M**16

D510**M**17

D510**M**18

D510**M**19
Daisies

General
- Flowers
  continued

D510N01

D510N02

D510N03

- Oak Leaves
- Acorns

D510N04

D510N05

D510N06

D510N07

Note: All images
are available as
fully editable vector
image files: see
page 286 or www.
ultimatesymbol.com

D510N08

D510N09
Oak Branch
Victory

D510N10

D510N11

Holly

D510**P**01
Poinsettia
Christmas

D510**P**02

D510**P**03

D510**P**04

D510**P**05

D510**P**06

D510**P**07

D510**P**10

D510**P**08

D510**P**09

D510**P**11

D510**P**12

D510**P**13

D510**P**14

D510**P**15

D510**P**16

D510**P**17

11

General

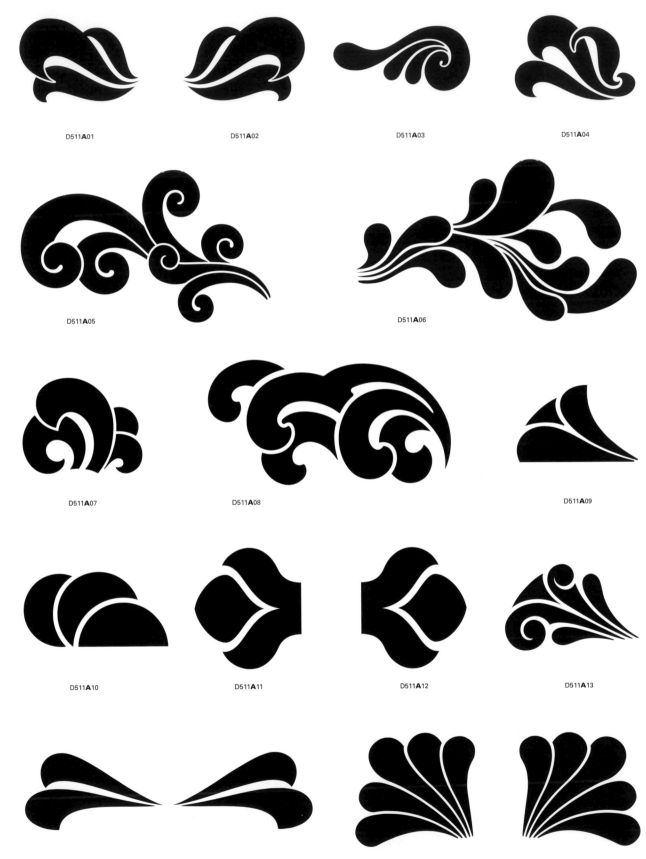

D511**A**01

D511**A**02

D511**A**03

D511**A**04

D511**A**05

D511**A**06

D511**A**07

D511**A**08

D511**A**09

D511**A**10

D511**A**11

D511**A**12

D511**A**13

D511**A**14

D511**A**15

D511**A**16

D511**A**17

General
continued

D511**B**01

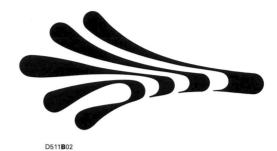

D511**B**02

D511**B**03

D511**B**04

D511**B**05

D511**B**06

D511**B**07

D511**B**08

D511**B**09

D511**B**10

General
continued

D511**C**01

D511**C**02

D511**C**03

D511**C**04

D511**C**05

D511**C**06

D511**C**07

D511**C**08

Note: All images
are available as
fully editable vector
image files: see
page 286 or www.
ultimatesymbol.com

D511**C**09

D511**C**10

General
continued

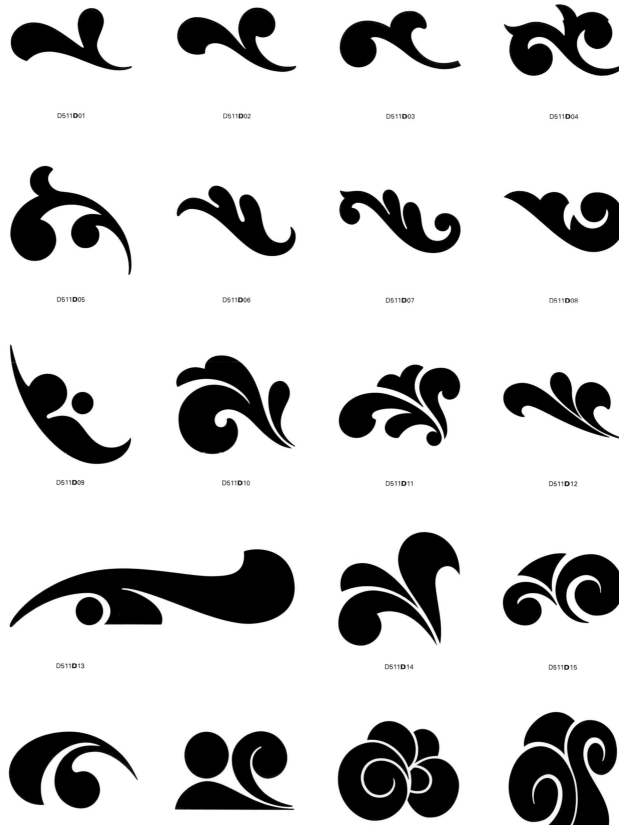

D511**D**01

D511**D**02

D511**D**03

D511**D**04

D511**D**05

D511**D**06

D511**D**07

D511**D**08

D511**D**09

D511**D**10

D511**D**11

D511**D**12

D511**D**13

D511**D**14

D511**D**15

D511**D**16

D511**D**17

D511**D**18

D511**D**19

General
continued

D511E01

D511E02

D511E03

D511E04

D511E05

D511E06

D511E07

D511E08

D511E09

D511E10

D511E11

D511E12

D511E13

D511E14

D511E15

D511E16

General
continued

D511F01

D511F02

D511F03

D511F04

D511F05

D511F06

D511F07

D511F08

D511F09

D511F10

D511F11

D511F12

D511F13

D511F14

D511F15

D511F16

D511F17

General
continued

D511**G**01

D511**G**02

D511**G**03

D511**G**04

D511**G**05

D511**G**06

D511**G**07

D511**G**08

D511**G**09

D511**G**10

D511**G**11

D511**G**12

D511**G**13

D511**G**14

D511**G**15

D511**G**16

D511**G**17

D511**G**18

D511**G**19

D511**G**20

General
continued

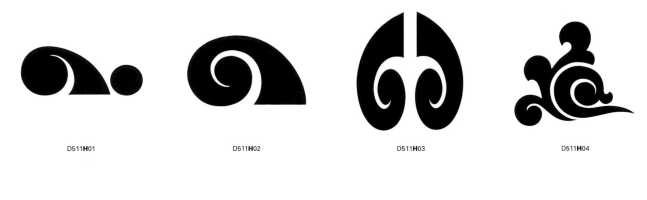

D511H01   D511H02   D511H03   D511H04

D511H05   D511H06   D511H07

D511H08   D511H09

D511H10   D511H11

D511H12   D511H13

Art Nouveau

D511J01   D511J02

D511J03   D511J04

D511J05   D511J06

D511J07   D511J08

D511J09   D511J10

D511J11   D511J12

Art Nouveau
continued

D511**K**01

D511**K**02

D511**K**03

D511**K**04

D511**K**05

D511**K**06

D511**K**07

D511**K**08

D511**K**09

D511**K**10

D511**K**11

D511**K**12

D511**K**13

D511**K**14

D511**K**15

D511**K**16

D511**K**17

D511**K**18

Art Nouveau
continued

D511L01

D511L02

D511L03

D511L04

D511L05

D511L06

D511L07

D511L08

D511L09

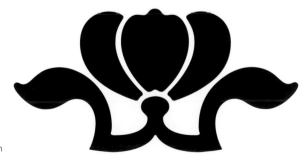

D511L10

D511L11

Art Nouveau
continued

D511**M**01

D511**M**02

D511**M**05

D511**M**03

D511**M**04

D511**M**06

D511**M**07

D511**M**08

D511**M**09

D511**M**10

D511**M**11

D511**M**12

12

Splashes
Splatters
Droplets

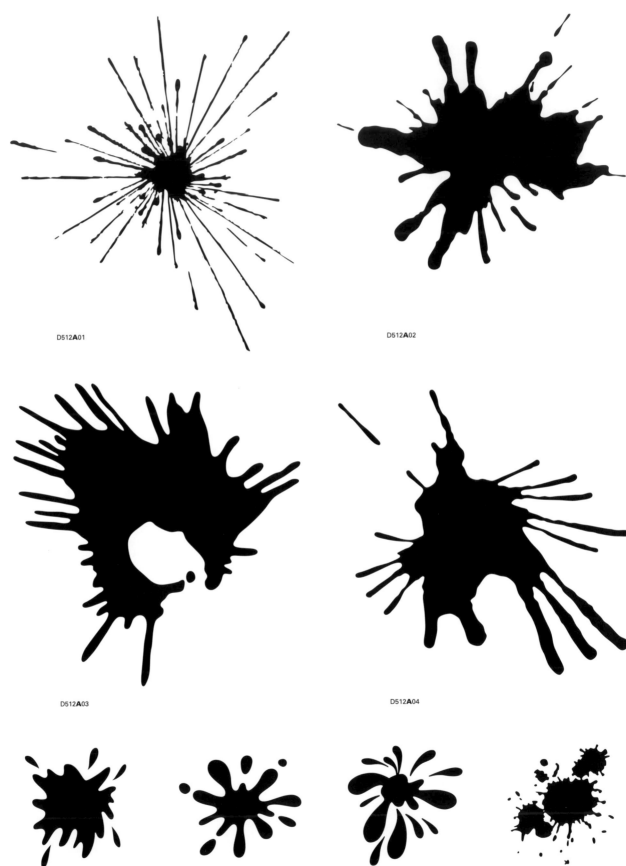

D512**A**01

D512**A**02

D512**A**03

D512**A**04

D512**A**05

D512**A**06

D512**A**07

D512**A**08

Splashes
Splatters
Droplets
continued

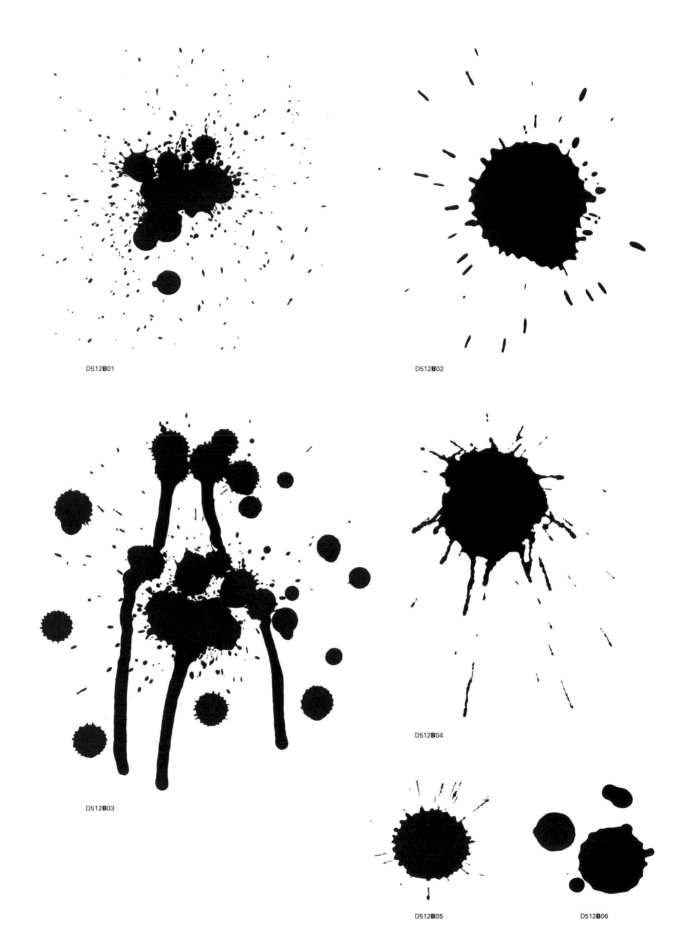

D512**B**01

D512**B**02

D512**B**03

D512**B**04

D512**B**05

D512**B**06

Droplets
continued
Drips

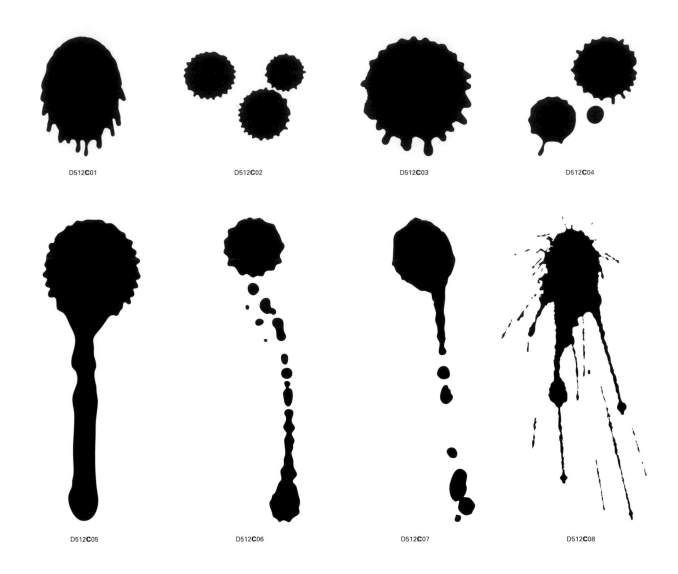

D512**C**01   D512**C**02   D512**C**03   D512**C**04

D512**C**05   D512**C**06   D512**C**07   D512**C**08

Note: All images
are available as
fully editable vector
image files: see
page 286 or www.
ultimatesymbol.com

D512**C**09   D512**C**10

Drips
continued

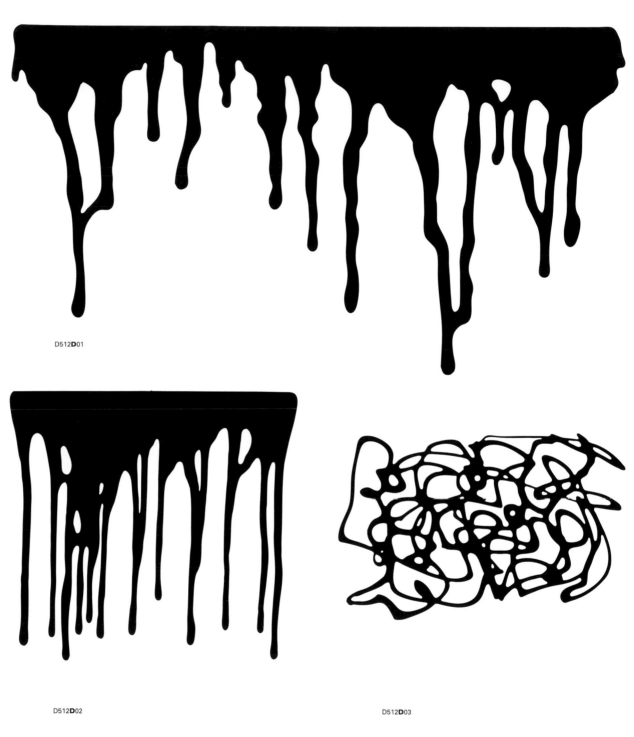

D512**D**01

D512**D**02   D512**D**03

Droplets

D512**D**04   D512**D**05

Brush Strokes

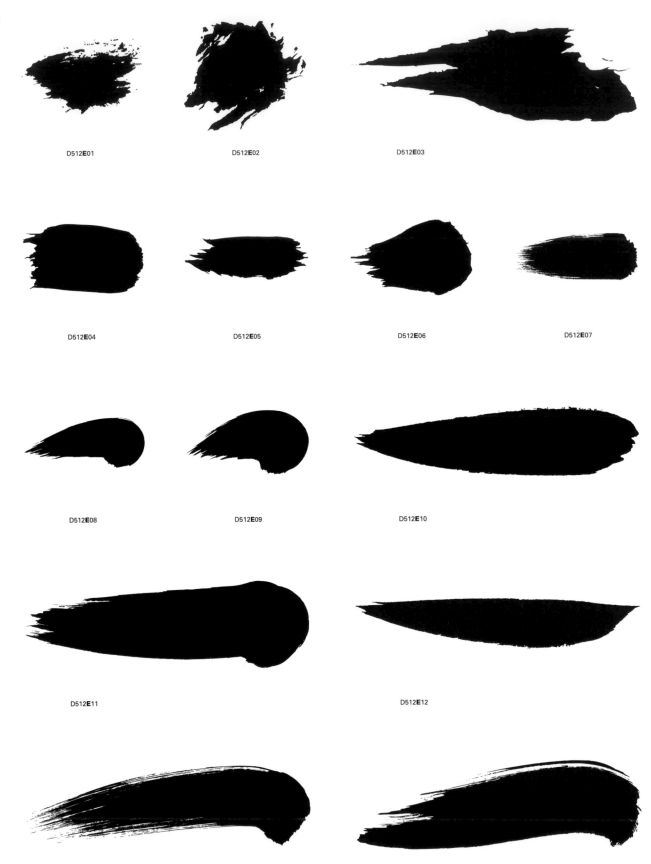

D512E01

D512E02

D512E03

D512E04

D512E05

D512E06

D512E07

D512E08

D512E09

D512E10

D512E11

D512E12

D512E13

D512E14

Brush Strokes
continued

D512**F**01

D512**F**02

D512**F**03

D512**F**04

D512**F**05

D512**F**06

D512**F**07

D512**F**08

D512**F**09

Brush Strokes
continued

D512**G**01

D512**G**02

D512**G**03

D512**G**04

D512**G**05

D512**G**06

D512**G**07

D512**G**08

D512**G**09

Brush Strokes
continued
- Squiggles

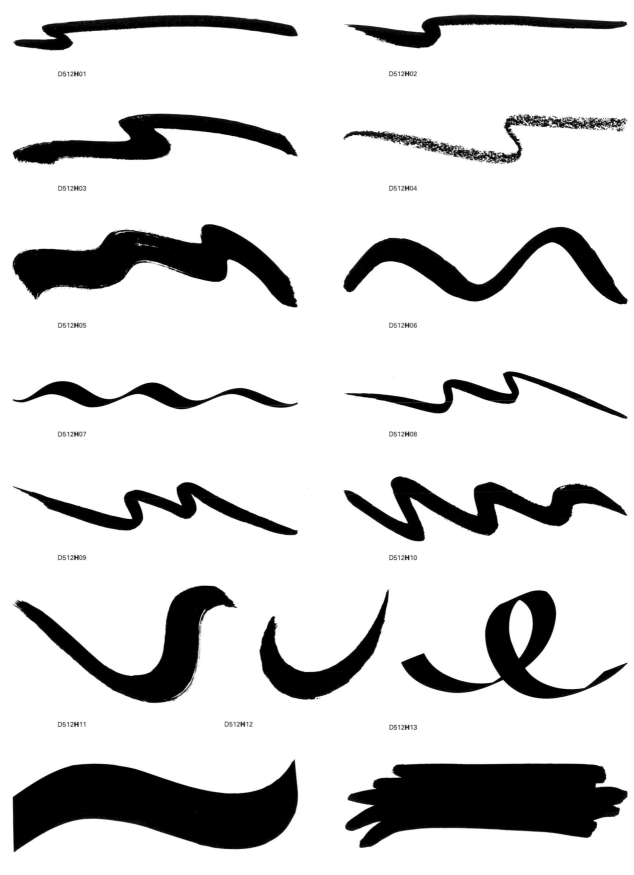

D512H01

D512H02

D512H03

D512H04

D512H05

D512H06

D512H07

D512H08

D512H09

D512H10

D512H11

D512H12

D512H13

D512H14

D512H15

Brush Strokes
continued
- Squiggles

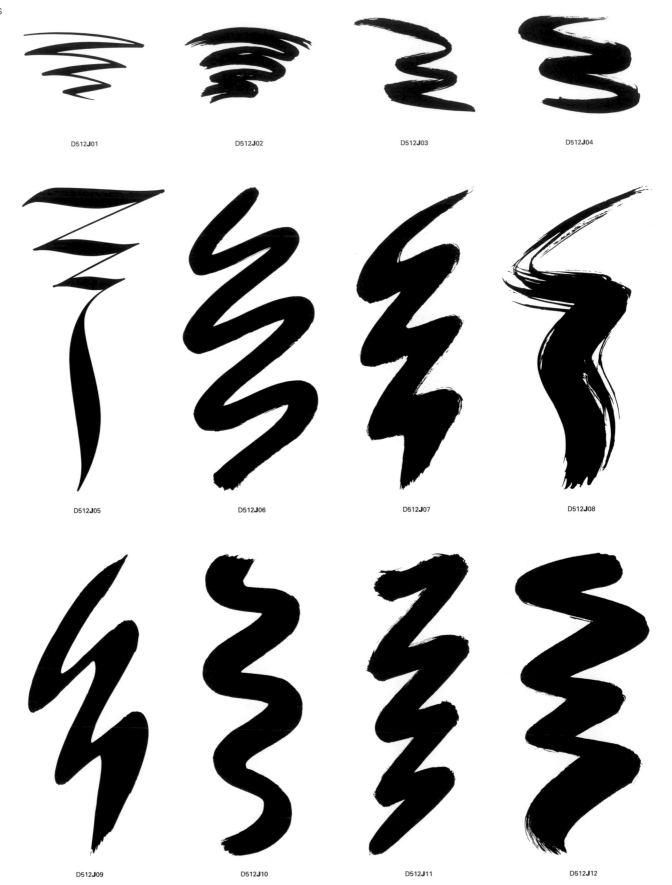

D512J01   D512J02   D512J03   D512J04

D512J05   D512J06   D512J07   D512J08

D512J09   D512J10   D512J11   D512J12

Brush Strokes
continued
- Squiggles

D512**K**01

D512**K**02

D512**K**03

D512**K**04

D512**K**05

D512**K**06

D512**K**07

D512**K**08

D512**K**09

D512**K**10

D512**K**11

D512**K**12

Spirals

D512L01

D512L02

D512L03

D512L04

D512L05

D512L06

D512L07

D512L08

D512L09

D512L10

D512L11

D512L12

D512L13

D512L14

D512L15

Blurbs

Circles

Infinity Loops

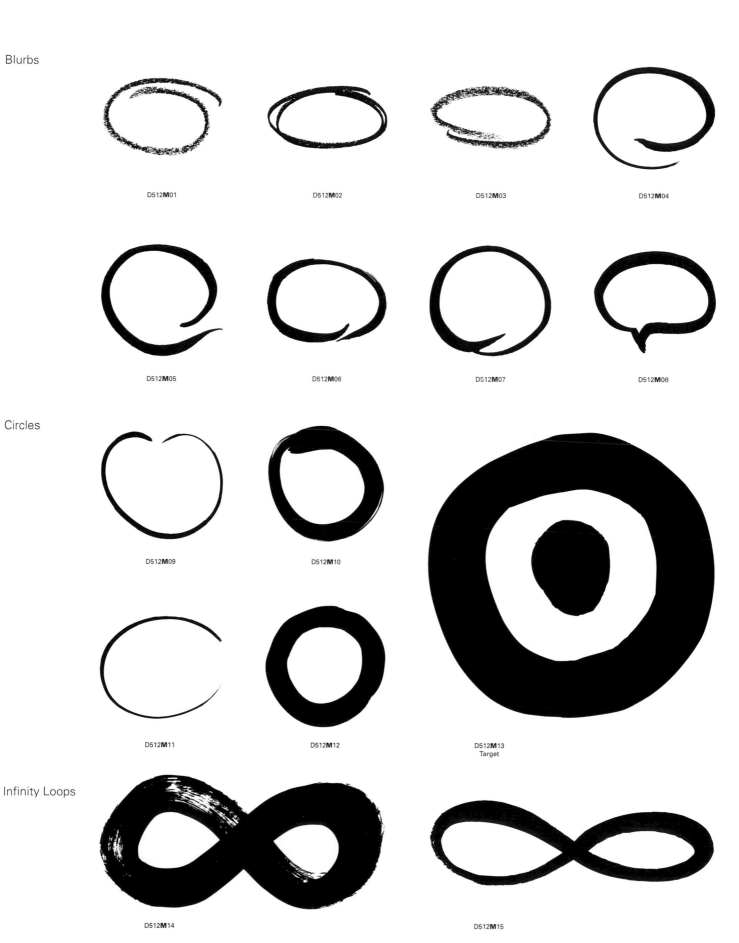

D512M01

D512M02

D512M03

D512M04

D512M05

D512M06

D512M07

D512M08

D512M09

D512M10

D512M11

D512M12

D512M13
Target

D512M14

D512M15

Triangles

Squares

Hearts

Drops

D512N01

D512N02

D512N03

D512N04

D512N05

D512N06

D512N07

D512N08

D512N09

D512N10

D512N11

D512N12

D512N13

D512N14

D512N15

D512N16

D512N17

Stars

Eyes

D512**P**01

D512**P**02

D512**P**03

D512**P**04

D512**P**05

D512**P**06

D512**P**07

D512**P**08

D512**P**09
Moon

D512**P**10

D512**P**11

D512**P**12

D512**P**13

D512**P**14

D512**P**15

D512**P**16

Suns

D512Q01

D512Q02

D512Q03

D512Q04

D512Q05
Sunset

Flowers

D512Q06

D512Q07

D512Q08

D512Q09

D512Q10

D512Q11

D512Q12

D512Q13

D512Q14

D512Q15

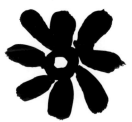

D512Q16

D512Q17

Asterisks

Crosses
X's

D512**R**01

D512**R**02

D512**R**03

D512**R**04

D512**R**05

D512**R**06

D512**R**07

D512**R**08

D512**R**09

D512**R**10

D512**R**11

D512**R**12

D512**R**13

D512**R**14

Crosses
X's
continued

D512S01

D512S02

D512S03

D512S04

D512S05

D512S06

D512S07
Number Sign

D512S08
Number Sign

D512S09

Dollar Signs
G-Clefs

D512S10

D512S11

D512S12

D512S13

D512S14

Question
Marks

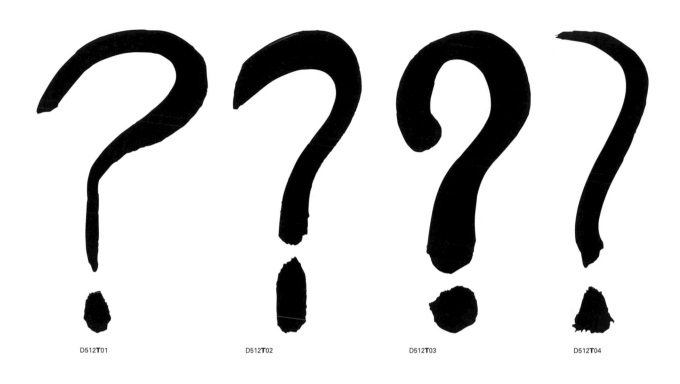

D512**T**01   D512**T**02   D512**T**03   D512**T**04

Exclamation
Marks

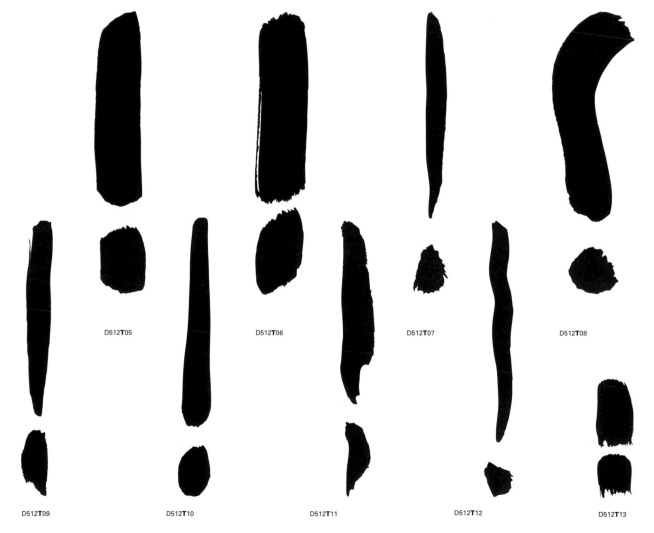

D512**T**05   D512**T**06   D512**T**07   D512**T**08

D512**T**09   D512**T**10   D512**T**11   D512**T**12   D512**T**13

Check Marks

Wings
Clouds

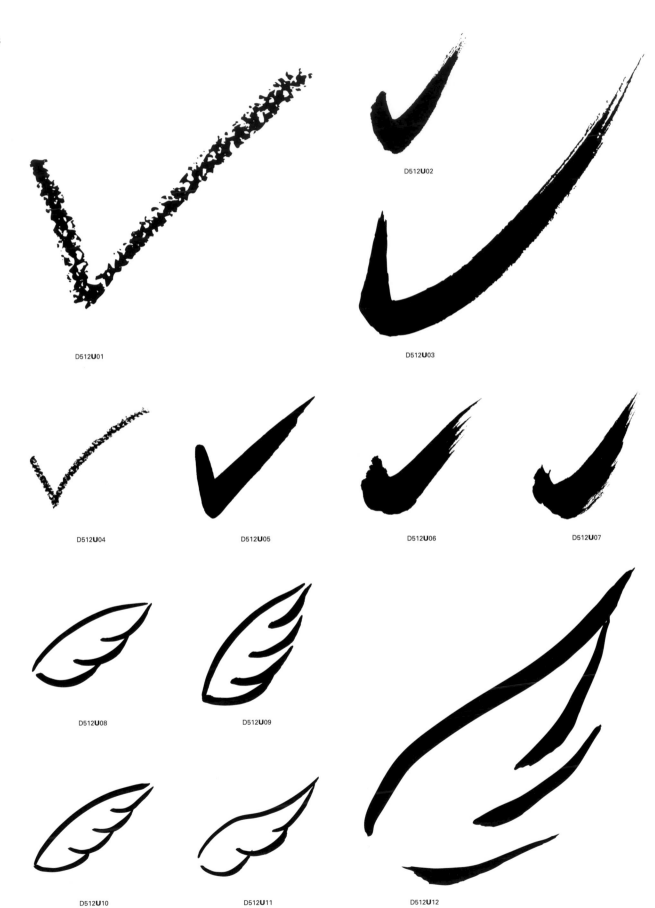

D512**U**01

D512**U**02

D512**U**03

D512**U**04

D512**U**05

D512**U**06

D512**U**07

D512**U**08

D512**U**09

D512**U**10

D512**U**11

D512**U**12

Arrows

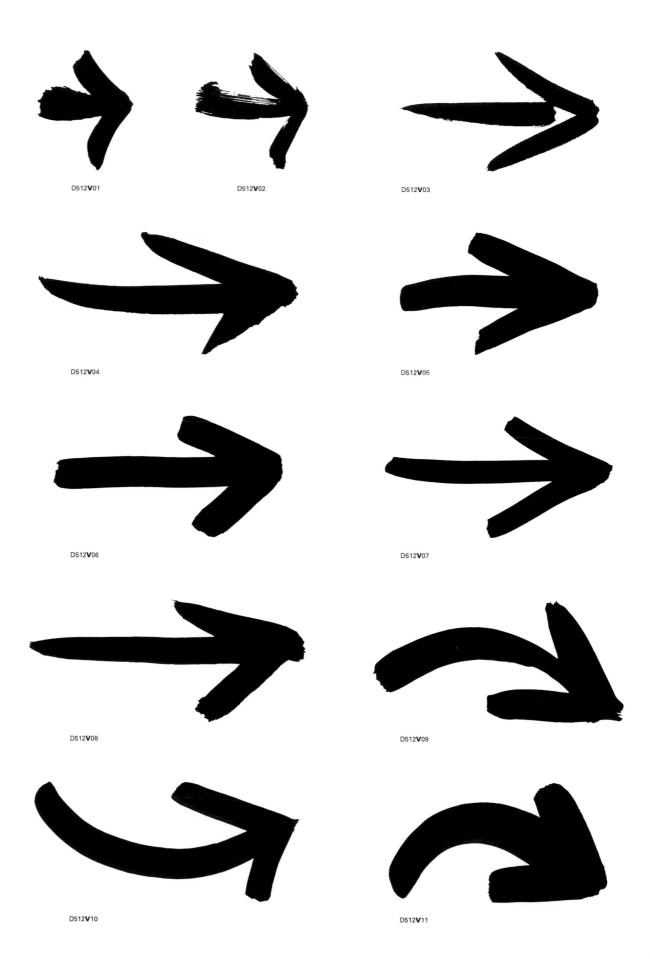

D512**V**01

D512**V**02

D512**V**03

D512**V**04

D512**V**05

D512**V**06

D512**V**07

D512**V**08

D512**V**09

D512**V**10

D512**V**11

Torn Paper

D512**W**01   D512**W**02   D512**W**03   D512**W**04   D512**W**05

Cut Paper
Torn Spiral
Binder Paper

D512**X**01   D512**X**02   D512**X**03   D512**X**04

13

General

D513A01

D513A02

D513A03

D513A04

D513A05

D513A06

D513A07

D513A08

D513A09

Typographic

D513B01   D513B02   D513B03   D513B04

D513B05   D513B06   D513B07   D513B08

D513B09   D513B10   D513B11   D513B12

D513B13   D513B14   D513B15   D513B16

D513B17   D513B18   D513B19   D513B20

Numerals

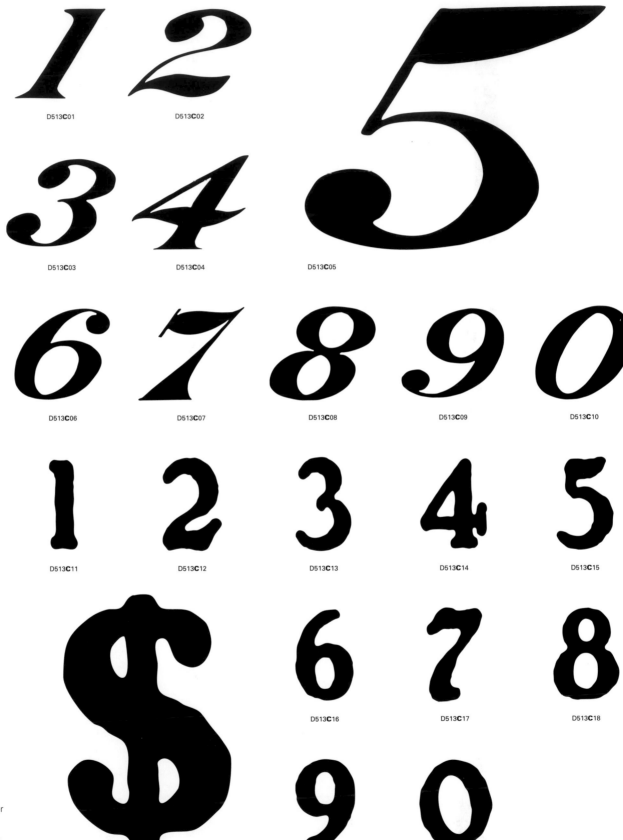

D513**C**01   D513**C**02

D513**C**03   D513**C**04   D513**C**05

D513**C**06   D513**C**07   D513**C**08   D513**C**09   D513**C**10

D513**C**11   D513**C**12   D513**C**13   D513**C**14   D513**C**15

D513**C**16   D513**C**17   D513**C**18

Note: All images
are available as
fully editable vector
image files: see
page 286 or www.
ultimatesymbol.com

D513**C**19   D513**C**20   D513**C**21

Numerals
continued

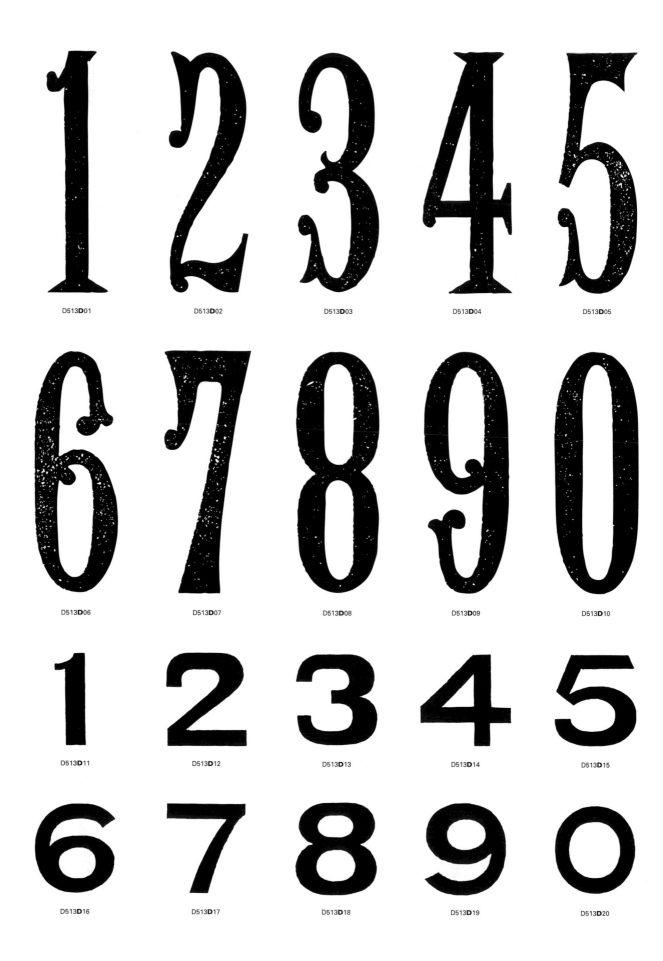

D513**D**01　　D513**D**02　　D513**D**03　　D513**D**04　　D513**D**05

D513**D**06　　D513**D**07　　D513**D**08　　D513**D**09　　D513**D**10

D513**D**11　　D513**D**12　　D513**D**13　　D513**D**14　　D513**D**15

D513**D**16　　D513**D**17　　D513**D**18　　D513**D**19　　D513**D**20

Numerals
continued

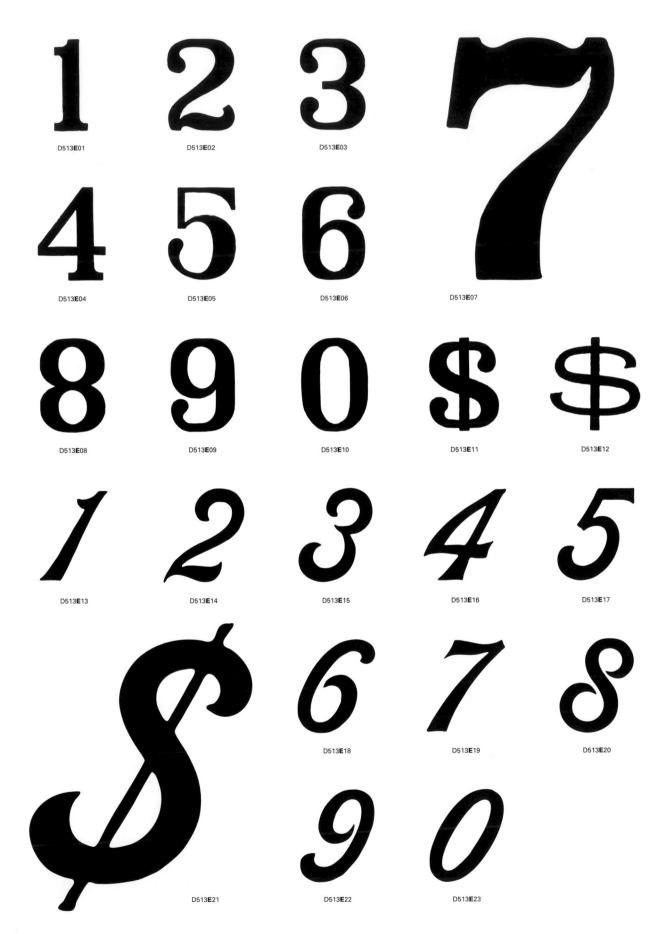

D513E01

D513E02

D513E03

D513E04

D513E05

D513E06

D513E07

D513E08

D513E09

D513E10

D513E11

D513E12

D513E13

D513E14

D513E15

D513E16

D513E17

D513E18

D513E19

D513E20

D513E21

D513E22

D513E23

Numerals

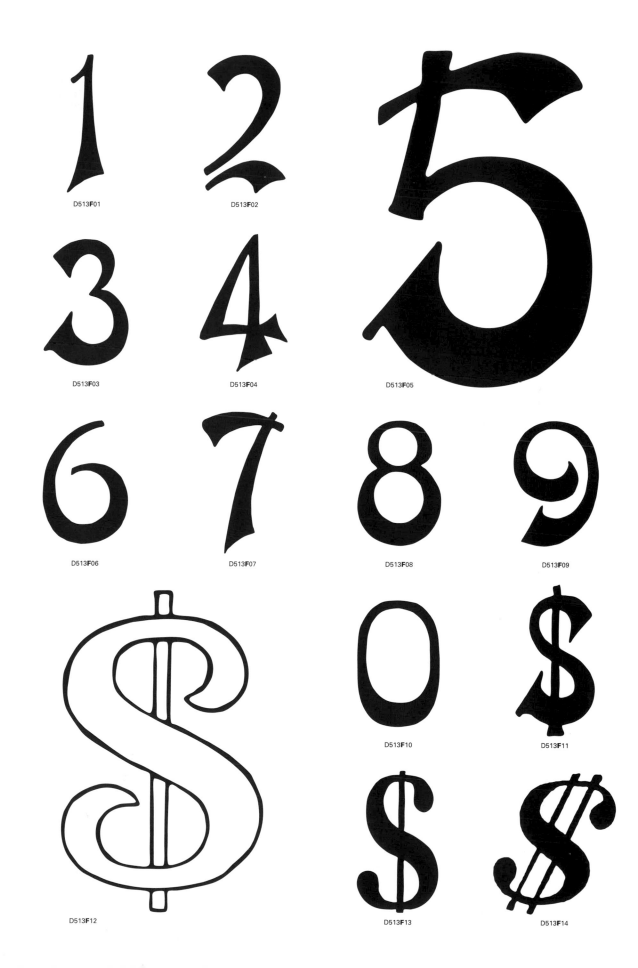

D513F01

D513F02

D513F03

D513F04

D513F05

D513F06

D513F07

D513F08

D513F09

D513F10

D513F11

D513F12

D513F13

D513F14

General

D513**G**01

D513**G**02

D513**G**03

D513**G**04

D513**G**05

D513**G**06

D513**G**07

D513**G**08

D513**G**09

- Finance

D513**G**10

D513**G**11

D513**G**12

D513**G**13

D513**G**14

D513**G**15

D513**G**16

D513**G**17

D513**G**18

D513**G**19

D513**G**20

D513**G**21

Finance
continued

D513H01

D513H02

D513H03

D513H04

D513H05

D513H06

D513H07

D513H08

D513H09

D513H10

D513H11

D513H12

D513H13

D513H14

D513H15

D513H16

D513H17

Finance
continued

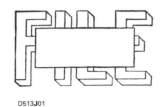

D513J01

D513J02

D513J03

D513J04

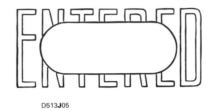

D513J05

D513J06

D513J07

D513J08

D513J09

Postal Motifs
- Envelopes
- Stamps
- Cancellations

D513J10
Envelope

D513J11
Envelope

D513J12
Envelope

D513J13

D513J14

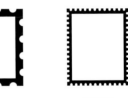

D513J15

D513J16

D513J17

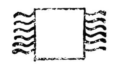

D513J18

D513J19

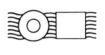

D513J20

D513J21

D513J22

D513J23

D513J24

D513J25

Note: All images
are available as
fully editable vector
image files: see
page 286 or www.
ultimatesymbol.com

D513J26

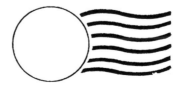

D513J27

D513J28

Postal Motifs
continued
- Stamps
- Cancellations

D513**K**01

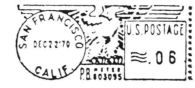

D513**K**02

D513**K**03

D513**K**04

D513**K**05

D513**K**06

D513**K**07   D513**K**08

D513**K**09

D513**K**10

D513**K**11

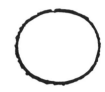

D513**K**12

D513**K**13
Par Avion
Lotnicza

D513**K**14
Par Avion
Luftpost

D513**K**15
Fragile

D513**K**16
Express

D513**K**17
First Class

D513**K**18
Third Class

D513**K**19
Parcel Post

D513**K**20
Special Delivery

D513**K**21
C.O.D.

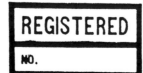

D513**K**22
Registered

D513**K**23
Returned to Sender

D513**K**24
U.S. Mail

LOOK ME

IN

Ultimate
Symbol™

**Design Elements 5™
by Ultimate Symbol**

©2007 Ultimate Publishing v5.0 Mac

CD

Overview

Welcome to *Design Elements 5:* This 13-volume collection of 5,025 high-quality vector files was created by design professionals *for* design professionals. *Design Elements 5* is part of *The Ultimate Symbol Collection*, a suite of products that provides instant access to a wide variety of inspirational, high-quality, and time-saving designs and icons, in fully editable PostScript™ format. For more about what products are available, please visit www.ultimatesymbol.com

This section contains the following information:

> Product Contents
> CD License
> CD Warranty
> Locating Image Files
> About EPS Files
> Vinyl-ready for Signmaking
> Opening EPS Files
> Display Problems
> Transparency & Compound Paths
> Images Composed of Separate Shapes
> About Adobe Acrobat Reader
> Ordering & Upgrades

PRODUCT CONTENTS
MAC or PC CD-ROM

1. EPS Files

EPS 3.0 format for Mac or PC. These files are non-application specific, meaning that they will function in almost any application that accepts postscript art.

Vinyl-Ready Signmaking Files The EPS 3.0 files in Mac or PC format on the CD-ROMs were designed specifically for sign making applications and vinyl sign cutting. The images have no strokes or overlapping vectors and points. For more information see page 285.

2. End User License Agreement

By using the images on the *Design Elements 5* CD-ROM, you agree to the terms and conditions of this agreement (located on pages 283-284 of this book).

4. Adobe Acrobat Reader™

An intuitive screen interface and image browser. Install to view the PDF documents listed below.

5. DE5 Catalog.pdf

On-screen display of the *Design Elements 5 Catalog* may be viewed in Adobe Acrobat Reader.

6. Ultimate Symbol.pdf

An overview of *The Ultimate Symbol Collection*™, a library of more than 25,000 images. Use to view and access the Free Sample Files.

7. FREE Sample Files

FREE sample EPS files from some of the other available products in *The Ultimate Symbol Collection*.

Notice to User:
This is a contract. By breaking the seal on the CD-ROM that accompanies this book, you accept all the terms and conditions of this agreement.

LICENSE AGREEMENT

Software Use: Ultimate Symbol grants you a non-exclusive limited license to use the EPS Files on one Apple Macintosh or IBM/PC compatible computer. You may not install the EPS Files on a network server. You may use the EPS Files as illustrative or decorative material that is included as part of a total graphic design for print or multimedia communication, produced for you, your employer, or a client, that is not for resale or redistribution as a collection of art for reproduction or as any form of stock design. You may not use any of the contents, in whole or in part, for multiple resale in the form of stock proofs, engravings, film, mats, printing, digitized images, etc. without written permission. When using an outside service bureau or high resolution output service, one copy of the EPS image or images may be made to accompany the document in which the images have been used. This copy is for one time use only and must be removed from the service bureau's possession upon completion of the service.

You may make one (1) copy of the EPS Files solely for backup purposes. Any permitted copies must include the same proprietary and copyright notices as were affixed to the original. Any unauthorized duplication or use of the EPS Files, in whole or in part, in print, or in any other storage and retrieval system is strictly prohibited.

Multi User License

If you plan to operate the EPS Files on a network or use simultaneously on multiple computers, contact Ultimate Symbol at 800.611.4761 regarding volume discounts and Multi User Licenses. If a Multi User License is obtained, only the number of copies needed to run the software simultaneously on the machines covered by Multi User License may be made.

Termination

Ultimate Symbol reserves the right to terminate this license upon breach. Upon termination, you will be required to cease using the EPS Files and return all copies of the EPS Files and accompanying documentation to Ultimate Symbol. In the event you include the EPS Files or any portion thereof, whether modified or not, in any other Software product for resale as "Clip-Art", this license is terminated and you agree to remove the EPS Files or any portion of them from the modified program and return it to Ultimate Symbol at the address listed below.

Copyright

The contents of the EPS Files and accompanying Documentation are the property of Ultimate Symbol and are copyrighted, with all rights reserved. Under the copyright laws, the EPS Files may not be copied, in whole or in part, without written consent of Ultimate Symbol, except to make a backup copy. This exception does not allow copies to be made for others, whether or not sold. Under the law, copying includes translating into another language or format. The purchase or use of this Software does not, in any way, transfer ownership or rights to contents, in whole or in part, to you. You are forewarned that Ultimate Symbol claims protection of the EPS Files and the symbols contained therein.

Transfer

You may not rent, lease, or sublicense, or lend the EPS Files or Documentation. You may, however, transfer all your rights to use the EPS Files to another person or legal entity provided that you transfer this Agreement and transfer (or destroy), the EPS Files, including all copies, updates and prior versions, and all Documentation to such person or entity and provided that you retain no copies, including copies stored on your computer.

Updates and Upgrades

Updates or upgrades of this software do not convey the right to transfer prior versions to other parties.

LIMITED WARRANTY

Ultimate Symbol warrants to the original purchaser of this Software that:

(1) this Software will perform substantially in accordance with the accompanying written materials, when used with the recommended system configuration, and

(2) the disk or disks upon which this Software is recorded are not defective and have been properly recorded.

90-Day Period

This warranty is for a period of 90 days after the original date of the purchaser's purchase of this package, during which time any disks that become defective under normal use will be replaced at no charge. The product must be registered with Ultimate Symbol in order to take advantage of this warranty.

Returned Goods Policy

Ultimate Symbol Customer Service must be notified before returning the Ultimate Symbol Software Product. Returned Software will not be accepted by Ultimate Symbol unless accompanied by a Returned Merchandise Authorization (RMA) number assigned by Ultimate Symbol Customer Service. Ultimate Symbol's entire liability under this limited warranty and otherwise with respect to the Software is limited to return of the Software and accompanying materials to the dealer or to Ultimate Symbol for replacement or refund, at Ultimate Symbol's option.

In no event shall Ultimate Symbol, its suppliers, employees, officers, directors, dealers, or distributors be liable for any damages, including lost profits or lost savings or other incidental or consequential damages, arising out of the use, inability to use, or abuse of this product, even if advised of the possibility of such damages, or for any claim by any other party.

Disclaimer

Ultimate Symbol disclaims all other warranties, either expressed or implied, including but not limited to implied warranties of merchantability and fitness for a particular purpose. Ultimate Symbol does not warrant that the functions contained in this Software will meet your requirements or that the operation of the Software will be uninterrupted or error free.

Some states do not allow limitations of implied warranties, or incidental or consequential damages, so some of the above limitations may not apply to you.

The images in this collection were created, compiled, and collected from a wide variety of sources. Some images were derived from reprinted, secondary or non-original sources. Every attempt has been made to verify that these images are copyright-free. However, in the event that an image has unknowingly infringed a copyright, please alert a representative of Ultimate Symbol at 800.611.4761.

LOCATING IMAGE FILES

Once you have found the image you want in the *Design Elements 5 Catalog*, take note of the number at the base of the image.

Example:

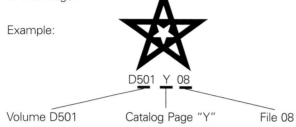

D501 Y 08

Volume D501   Catalog Page "Y"   File 08

To find the EPS image, select your CD-ROM drive and locate the EPS Files folder. Then locate the folder entitled Volume D501, Sub-folder D501Y, File Number D501Y08.

ABOUT EPS FILES

Design Elements 5 images are vector outlines, and will print at the very highest resolution on any Post-Script™-equipped printer. These images were created in Adobe Illustrator and saved as grouped, 1-bit, Adobe Illustrator 3.0 EPS files in both Macintosh and PC/Windows formats. The images were not saved in higher versions of Illustrator because of backward compatibility issues.

VINYL-READY FOR SIGNMAKING

The images are vinyl-ready and were designed specifically for use by signmakers: they have no strokes (in most cases), or overlapping vectors and points. Exceptions include outlines for some surround shapes, which can either be deleted or altered to conform with your sign application(s).

Opening EPS Files

You may edit these in any draw or sign making program that accepts EPS files, such as *Adobe Illustrator*™, *CorelDRAW!*™, *Arts & Letters Express*™, *CASmate*™, *EuroCUT*™, *FlexiSIGN*™, *GERBER Graphix Advantage*™, and place or import them into most page layout programs, such as *Quark Express*™, *Adobe InDesign*™, *Adobe Pagemaker*™, etc. For up-to-date instructions on opening or importing EPS files, use "Help" menus or contact the application manufacturer's tech support.

Display Problems

If you encounter "jaggies" when viewing the images on screen and they appear roughly drawn, check and/or update your computer's Adobe PostScript drivers or make sure that the application you are working in is PostScript-compatible.

Transparency & Compound Paths

Where appropriate, 3.0 images were saved as compound paths, which allows for transparency or the ability to "see through" blank areas of the image (below left).

If a grouped image will not come apart, it may be because the file is a compound path. To release a compound path in Illustrator, select the image, pull down the "Object" menu, select "Compound Path", then select "Release". Be aware that when releasing a compound path, some apparently empty or transparent objects/spaces may become solid black or white (example, above right).

Images Composed of Separate Shapes

Many of the images in *Design Elements 5* are composed of separate, grouped shapes which may be pulled apart. In particular, if an image appears in the catalog with an asterisk * in the lower right corner, it is composed of separate, overlapping shapes. To decompose the image, select the image, go to "Object" menu, and select "Ungroup". You are now ready to pull it apart.

ABOUT ADOBE ACROBAT READER

With the Acrobat Reader, you can view and navigate any Portable Document Format (PDF) file, including our screen catalog "DE5 Catalog.pdf" (Mac); "DE5_Cat.pdf" (PC) and "Ultimate Symbol.pdf" (Mac); "Ultimate.pdf" (PC). For your convenience, a version of Acrobat Reader is provided in the "Acrobat Reader" folder on the CD-ROM (also available free from Adobe).

IMPORTANT: It is not necessary to load Acrobat Reader or our screen catalog "DE5 Catalog.pdf" to begin using the EPS files. However, the screen catalog will assist you in conveniently viewing and selecting the image files, with its search and bookmark capabilities. *Note that the DE5.pdf document is locked for copyright reasons and is therefore not printable.*

How to Purchase Electronic Artwork for the Symbols in this Book

All 5,025 symbols displayed in *Design Elements 5* are available as fully editable EPS vector image files for Mac or PC.

CD Upgrade Discount for Book Owners

If you already own the *Design Elements 5* Book, you qualify for a special CD upgrade discount. Please call to obtain your discount toll-free: 800.611.4761.

Online Purchases

www.ultimatesymbol.com
Follow instructions to purchase any of the following:

> Single Image Downloads

> Individual Volume Downloads

> *Design Elements 5,* Book with CD (shipped)

> *Design Elements 5,* CD only (shipped)

> *Design Elements 5,* Book only (shipped)

Multi-User Licensing

If you intend to use the *Design Elements 5* electronic art on more than one computer or on a network, please contact Ultimate Symbol for special multi-user licensing and multiple discount pricing.

Quantity Discounts

Special bulk purchase and educational discount rates are available. Please call 845.942.0003 for information.

Ultimate Symbol

31 Wilderness Drive
Stony Point, New York 10980-3447
800.611.4761
www.ultimatesymbol.com

Call Toll-Free: 800.611.4761

Monday through Friday, 10 am to 6 pm EST (Eastern Standard Time) for information, pricing, and ordering. Orders received by 1:00 pm EST usually ship same day.

Outside the U.S. Call: 845.429.0937

Order by Fax: 845.942.0004

24 hours a day, 7 days a week.
Please include name, address, email address, and phone number along with credit card number and expiration date. You will be contacted with any questions. Copies of your invoice will be emailed and included with shipped product.

Order by Mail

Please include name, address, email address, and phone number along with check, money order, or credit card number and expiration date. You will be contacted with any questions. Mail to:
Ultimate Symbol
Attn: Orders
31 Wilderness Drive
Stony Point, New York 10980-3447

Payment

Visit www.ultimatesymbol.com for current pricing.
Payment options include:
1. Credit Cards:
   MasterCard, Visa, American Express, Discover.
2. Checks:
   Corporate or personal (product ships only upon clearance of check).
3. Purchase Orders:
   Government and educational institutions only.
   Please call 845.942.0003 for more information.

Shipping & Delivery

Orders received by 1:00 pm EST usually ship same day and are tracked in the U.S. Sorry, no C.O.D. orders.
1. Overnight Priority (delivery by 10:30 am)
   Overnight Standard (delivery by 3:00 pm)
2. Two-Day Economy
3. Ground (1-7 days)
4. Foreign: U.S. Postal Service International Priority Mail